SAMSUNG

A55 5G USER GUIDE

THE COMPLETE, STEP-BY-STEP MANUAL FOR BEGINNERS AND SENIORS TO GET STARTED WITH, AND MASTER THE NEW GALAXY A55 5G PHONE LIKE A PRO WITH CAMERA TIPS AND TRICKS

BENJAMIN ISRAEL

Copyright © 2024 BENJAMIN ISRAEL

Disclaimer: This book is not an official Samsung Galaxy manual. The images used in this manual are only for illustrative purposes; all information is deemed accurate and meant to assist the reader/user. The author/publisher shall not be liable for any misuse, abuse, damage, or loss arising from applying any of the contents in this manual. Please contact the carrier or manufacturer of your device if you have any queries or concerns.

All rights reserved. This book is copyright and no part of it may be reproduced, distributed, or transmitted in any form or by any means, including photocopying, recording, or other electronic or mechanical methods, without the prior written permission of the publisher, except in the case of brief quotations embodied in critical reviews and certain other noncommercial uses permitted by copyright law.

Printed in the United States of America

Copyright © 2024 BENJAMIN ISRAEL

Contents

INTRODUCTION 1
CHAPTER 1: 3
GETTING STARTED 3
   Device layout and features.. 3
   Physical (Hard) buttons and their functions........ 6
      How to set the Side button 6
   Soft buttons and their functions............................. 7
   How to charge the battery 8
      Wired charging 8
      Quick charging 8
      How to charge other devices................................. 9
      Reducing the battery consumption 9
      Battery charging tips and precautions........... 10
   How to activate an eSIM and install a nano-SIM card 11
      Steps for installing the SIM or USIM card 12
      How to activate an eSIM on your Galaxy A55 5G... 14

SIM card manager (dual SIM models) 14

How to insert an SD card 15

    How to safely remove an SD card from your Galaxy A55 5G 18

    Formatting the microSD card 19

How to turn on and off the Galaxy A55 5G 19

    Forcing restart 21

    Emergency mode 22

CHAPTER 2: 23

SETTING UP YOUR DEVICE 23

    Initial setup 23

How to set up Samsung account on your Galaxy A55 5G 23

    How to Find your ID and reset your password 24

    Signing out of your Samsung account 24

Transferring data from your previous device to your new Galaxy A55 5G(Smart Switch) 25

    Transferring data using a USB cable 25

    How to Transfer your data wirelessly 26

How to use external storage to backup and restore data 28

Transferring backup data from a computer to your new Galaxy A55 5G 28

Face recognition 30

Fingerprint recognition 33

Samsung Pay 38

How to Set up Samsung Pay on your Galaxy A55 5G Smartphone 39

Registering cards 40

How to manage your cards 42

How to view the last four-digit number of your cards 43

How to delete card from your Samsung pay 45

Making payments 46

Samsung Pass 47

How to install or uninstall apps on your new Galaxy A55 5G 50

Galaxy Store 50

Play Store 51

Managing apps 51

CHAPTER 3 53

BASIC FEATURES AND FUNCTIONS............................53

Understanding the screen 53

Navigation bar (soft buttons)................................54

Home screen and Apps screen..............................55

Edge panel 61

Lock screen 61

Indicator icons 62

Notification panel 64

Using quick setting buttons..................................65

Controlling media playback..................................66

Entering text..67

Keyboard layout..67

Copying and pasting...69

CHAPTER 4 71

COMMUNICATIONS..71

The Phone app 71

Making calls 71

Receiving calls 73

Blocking phone numbers 73

Options during calls 74

The Contacts app 75

Various ways to add contacts to your contact list on your Galaxy A55 5G 75

Searching for contacts 76

Sharing contacts 77

Creating groups 78

Merging duplicate contacts 78

The Messages app 78

Sending messages 78

Viewing messages 79

Changing message settings 80

Internet 80

Using secret mode 81

CHAPTER 5 83

THE CAMERA AND GALLERY APPS 83

Camera 83

How to take pictures with your Galaxy A55 5G 83

How to use the Photo mode on Galaxy A55 5G 90

Video mode 93

How to use the auto framing feature on your Galaxy A55 5G 94

How to record with Dual rec mode 94

    Portrait mode 95

    Fun mode 96

    Pro mode / Pro video mode 97

    Single take mode 99

    Night mode 100

    Food mode 100

    Panorama mode 100

    Macro mode 101

    Super Slow-mo mode 101

    Slow motion mode 102

    Hyperlapse mode 103

    Customizing camera settings 104

Creating events 129

Syncing events with your accounts 129

Reminder 130

Starting Reminder 130

Creating reminders 130

Completing reminders 131

Deleting reminders 131

Voice Recorder 131

Changing the recording mode on the Galaxy A55 5G 132

My Files 132

Gaming Hub 133

Removing a game from Gaming Hub 133

Changing the performance mode 133

Game Booster 134

Launching apps in pop-up windows while playing games 136

Google apps 136

CHAPTER 7 139

CONNECTIVITY AND SHARING 139

Wi-Fi 139

Bluetooth 141

NFC and contactless payments 144

Data saver 146

Allowed network for apps 147

Mobile Hotspot 148

More connection settings 149

Printing 149

Different ways to share content on your Galaxy A55 5G smartphone 151

How to use the Quick Share 151

Web link Sharing 154

Music Share 154

How to share your Bluetooth speaker with another device 155

Listening to music together with Galaxy Buds 156

SmartThings 157

Smart View 158

Link to Windows 158

Connecting to a computer 159
CHAPTER 8 161
CUSTOMIZATION SETTINGS 161
   Samsung account 161
   Notifications 161
   Display settings 162
      Motion smoothness 164
      How to change the screen mode or adjust the display color: 165
   Wallpaper 166
   Themes 166
CHAPTER 9 167
SETTINGS (PART 2) 167
   Home screen 167
   Lock screen 167
      Options 167
      Extended Unlock 168
      Always On Display 169
   Security and privacy 171
      Options 171

Secure Folder 173
Secure Wi-Fi 178

CHAPTER 10 181

MODES AND ROUTINES ON THE GALAXY A55 5G
.... 181

Adding modes 181
Running modes 181
Adding new routines 182
Running routines 182
Sounds and vibration 183
  Options 183
  Sound quality and effects 184
  Separate app sound 185

CHAPTER 11 187

ACCOUNTS AND BACKUP 187

Samsung Cloud 188

CHAPTER 12 190

ADVANCED SETTINGS 190

Advanced features 190
  Motions and gestures 191

Video call effects 192
Dual Messenger 193
Digital Wellbeing and parental controls 194
Battery and device care 195
Optimizing your device 195
Battery 196
Storage 197
Memory 197
App protection 198
Maintenance mode 198
How to use the Ultra data saving mode 198
Apps 199
General management 199
Adding device languages 200
Accessibility 201
Software update 202
Security updates information 202
About phone 202
CHAPTER 13 204

CARE AND MAINTENANCE TIPS 204

   Precautions for using the device 204

      Maintaining water and dust resistance 207

      Instructional icons 209

   Device overheating situations and solutions. 209

      When the device overheats during the process of charging the battery 209

      When the device heats up during use 210

      Precautions for device overheating 212

      Precautions for operating environment 213

CHAPTER 14 215

TROUBLESHOOTING TIPS 215

      Restarting the device 217

      Forcing restart 217

      Resetting the device 217

   Removing the battery 222

INDEX 224

INTRODUCTION

Congratulations on your purchase of the new Samsung Galaxy A55 5G smartphone! And welcome to the Galaxy Family" if this is your first Galaxy phone!!

The Samsung Galaxy A55 5G smartphone is a mid-range smartphone that blends the advanced features and functions, and good-feeling of the flagship series with affordability and availability.

The Galaxy A55 5G has a 6.6 inches screen, a Super AMOLED display of up to 120Hz refresh rate, Android 14, One UI 6.1 Operating System, powered by the Exynos 1480 chipset. It comes in two variants of 128GB and 256GB internal memory with a base RAM of 8GB and 12GB at the peak.

On the camera side, it showcases a triple camera system of 50MP wide, 12MP ultrawide, and 5MP macro cameras with support for 4K video recording.

Unfortunately, many users do not go beyond the basic functions of their smartphones – make and receive calls, send and receive text messages, browse the internet, play their favorite music, take some photos, and a few other things.

Having a brand-new gadget with cutting-edge features is great, but it's not everything.

The true value of your phone becomes apparent as you begin to know how to make the most out of its features in practical, day-to-day applications.

That's why this step-by-step guide is designed to help you get started with all the basic features and progress to master the advanced features, settings, and functions of your Galaxy A55 5G smartphone.

For photography enthusiasts, you've got a camera guide in it to spice up your digital photography experience.

In this manual, you'll also find useful tips on the care and maintain of your device, troubleshooting and a robust index to help you find whatever you're looking for.

So, shall we get started?

CHAPTER 1:
GETTING STARTED

Device layout and features

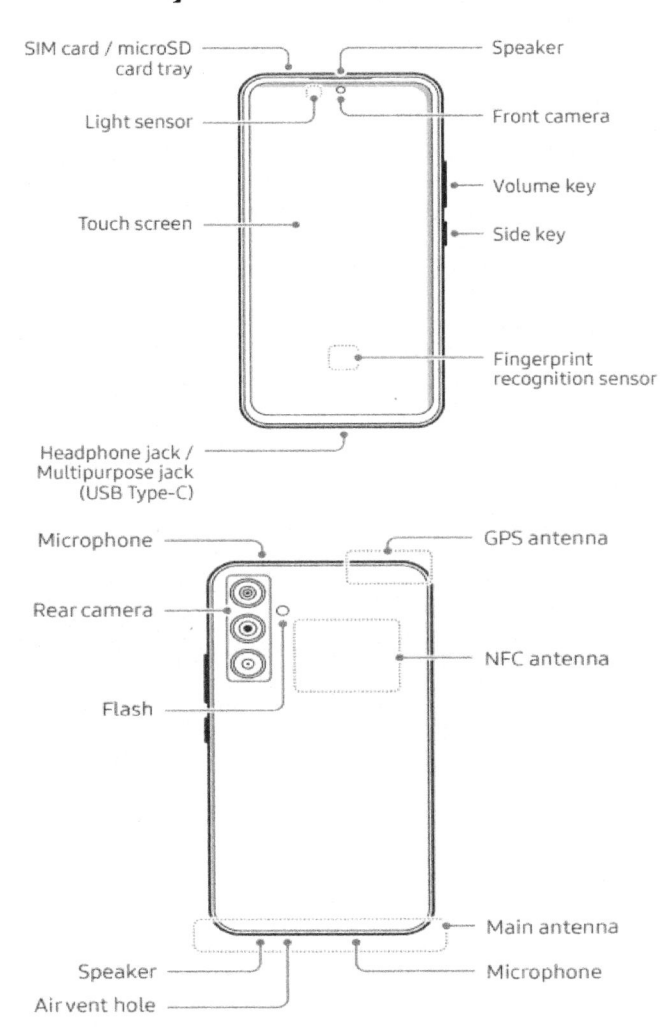

- SIM card / microSD card tray
- Speaker
- Light sensor
- Front camera
- Volume key
- Touch screen
- Side key
- Fingerprint recognition sensor
- Headphone jack / Multipurpose jack (USB Type-C)

- Microphone
- GPS antenna
- Rear camera
- NFC antenna
- Flash
- Main antenna
- Speaker
- Microphone
- Air vent hole

3

CAUTION:

- When using the speakers, such as when playing media files or using speakerphone, do not put the device near your ears.

- Take care not to expose the camera lens to a strong light source, such as direct sunlight as this may damage the camera image sensor. A damaged image sensor cannot be repaired and will produce dots or spots in pictures.

- If the device's glass or acrylic body is broken, take the device to a Samsung Service Centre for repairs before using it to avoid the risk of injury.

- If dust or foreign materials enter the microphone, speaker, or receiver, the device's sound may be impaired or certain features may not work. Attempting to remove the dust or foreign materials with a sharp object may cause damage to the device and affect its appearance.

NOTE:

- Connectivity problems and battery drain may ensue in the following circumstances:

- Attaching metallic stickers on the antenna area of the device
- Attaching a device cover made with metallic material to the device
- Shielding the device's antenna area with your hands or other objects as you're using certain features, such as calls or the mobile data connection
• It is advisable to use a Samsung-endorsed screen protector. The use of unapproved screen protectors may cause malfunctioning of the sensors.
• Never cover the light sensor area with screen accessories, such as a screen protector, stickers, or a cover as doing so may cause the sensor to malfunction.

Physical (Hard) buttons and their functions

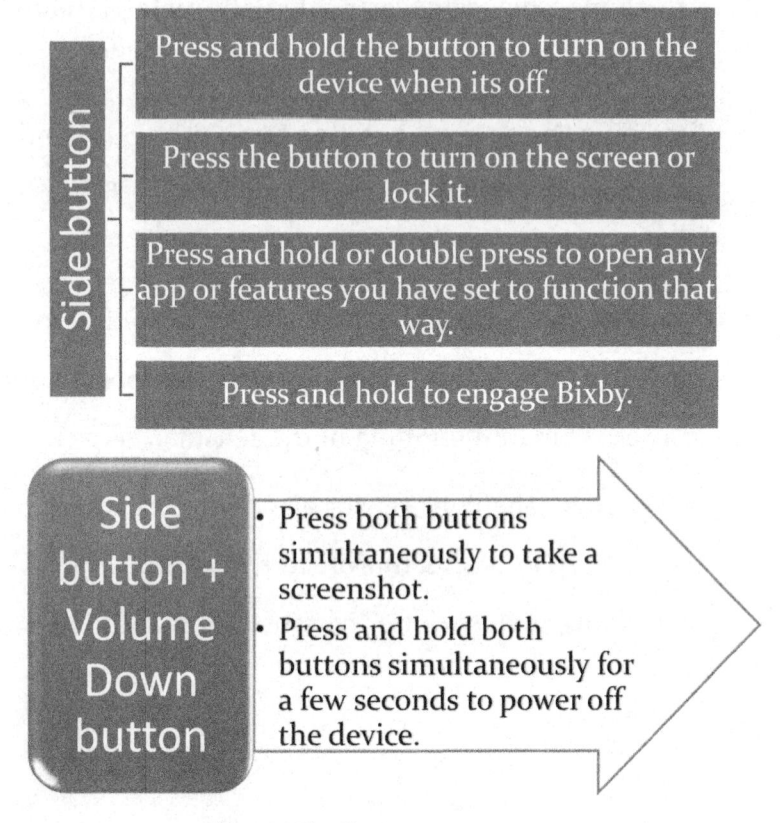

Side button
- Press and hold the button to turn on the device when its off.
- Press the button to turn on the screen or lock it.
- Press and hold or double press to open any app or features you have set to function that way.
- Press and hold to engage Bixby.

Side button + Volume Down button
- Press both buttons simultaneously to take a screenshot.
- Press and hold both buttons simultaneously for a few seconds to power off the device.

How to set the Side button

Choose the action to perform (e.g. an app or feature you want to open) anytime you double press the Side button or whenever you press down (i.e. press and hold) the Side button.

To do this, go to **Settings,** select **Advanced features,** select **Side button,** and then choose an option you want.

Soft buttons and their functions

The soft buttons are the navigation buttons that appear at the bottom of your device's screen whenever you turn it on.

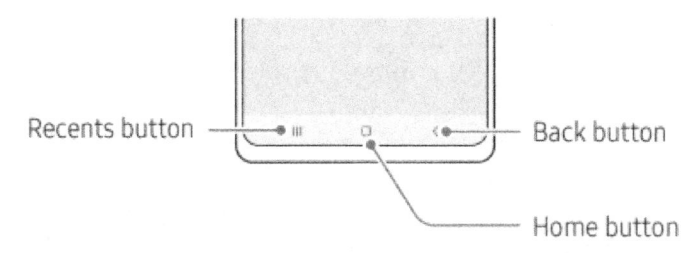

Recents button —— Back button

Home button

They give the user direction while operating the device, hence also called navigation buttons. As can be seen from the screenshot above, they are set to display the **Recents** button (left), **Home** button (center), and the **Back** button (right) on the navigation bar by default. However, you can also rearrange how they appear on the screen if you wish.

Their functions vary according to the current app being and as well as the usage environment. Below is an illustration of their general functions.

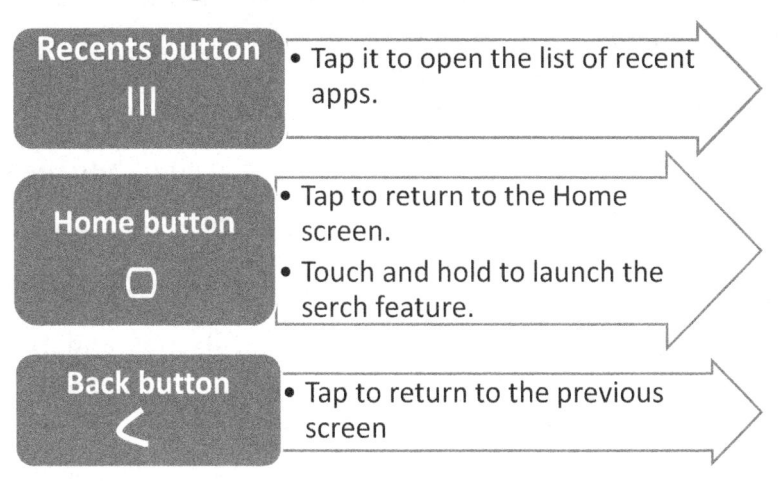

Recents button |||	• Tap it to open the list of recent apps.
Home button ☐	• Tap to return to the Home screen. • Touch and hold to launch the serch feature.
Back button <	• Tap to return to the previous screen

7

How to charge the battery

Charge the battery before using it for the first time or when it has been unused for prolonged periods.

Wired charging

Connect the device's USB cable to the USB power adaptor and plug the cable into the device's multipurpose jack to charge the battery. After the device is fully charged, disconnect the charger from the device.

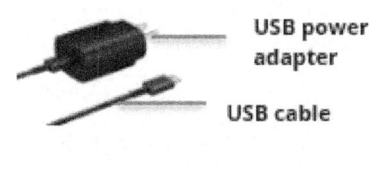

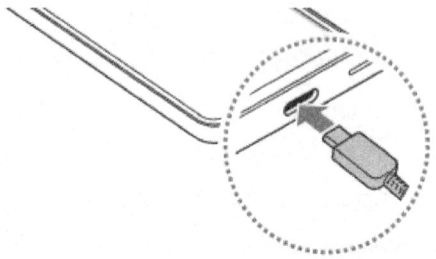

USB power adapter

USB cable

Quick charging

For quick charging, use a fast or super-fast charger.

To see if the charger is properly connected, go to **Settings** and tap **Battery**.

• If fast charging is not working, go to **Settings** > **Battery** > **Charging settings**. Confirm that the USB cord and the USB power adapter are securely connected as well.

- You can make the battery charge faster if you switch off the phone or its screen.

How to charge other devices

Charge another mobile device with your device's battery using the USB cable.

Connect your device and the other device using the USB cord that came with your device. Depending on the other device, a USB connection may be required.

When charging begins, the battery charging icon appears on the screen of the other device.

The app selection pop-up window that displays on your smartphone is meant for data transfer. Selecting an app from the pop-up window is not advised.

Reducing the battery consumption

Your smartphone offers various options that help you save battery power. These include:

- Activate power saving mode.
- Enhance the device using the device care feature.
- When the device is not being used, turn off the screen by pressing the Side key.
- Close unnecessary apps.

- Deactivate the Bluetooth feature when you're not using it.
- Reduce the backlight time.
- Reduce the screen brightness.
- Deactivate auto-syncing of apps which require syncing.

Battery charging tips and precautions

- If the battery is totally discharged, the device cannot be turned on instantly when the charger is connected. Allow an empty battery to charge for a few minutes before you turn on the device.
- If you use multiple apps at once, network apps, or apps that need a connection to another device, the battery will empty quickly. To avoid losing power during a data transfer, always use these apps after you've fully charged the battery.
- The charging speed of your device may reduce when you're charging it with other sources of power, e.g. a computer due to a lower electric current.
- The device can be used while charging, but it the battery may take longer time to get fully charged.

- If the device receives an unsteady power supply while charging, the touch screen may not work. In that case, disconnect the charger from the device.
- While charging, the device and the charger may become hot. This is normal and does not affect the device's lifespan or performance. However, if the battery gets hotter than normal, the charger may stop charging.
- If the multipurpose jack is wet and you use it to charge, it may cause damage to the device.
Always ensure the multipurpose jack is dry before charging the device.
- If the device is not charging appropriately, take the device and its charger to a Samsung Service Centre.

How to activate an eSIM and install a nano-SIM card

Insert the SIM or USIM card supplied by your service provider.

You can activate the embedded SIM (eSIM) or insert two physical SIM cards into the device if you want to use the same smartphone with two different phone numbers or providers. An embedded digital SIM card, or eSIM, is a different type of SIM card than a traditional nano-SIM card.

In some locations, using both the nano-SIM card and the eSIM may result in reduced data transmission speeds.

NOTE: Some services requiring a network connection may be unavailable depending on the service provider.

Steps for installing the SIM or USIM card

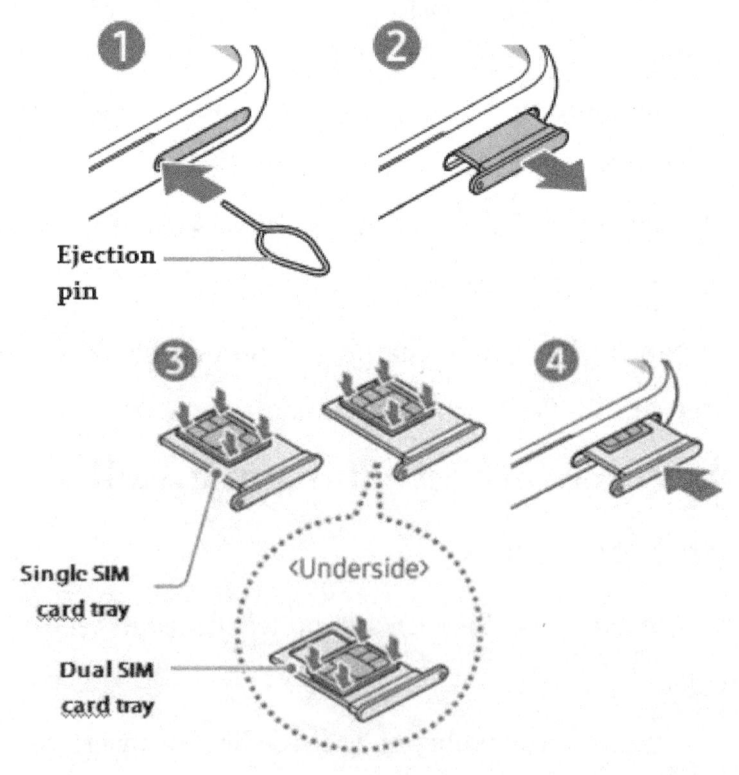

Ejection pin

Single SIM card tray

<Underside>

Dual SIM card tray

1. Push the ejection pin into the hole on the tray to bring out the tray.
2. Gently pull out the tray from the tray slot.

3   Put the SIM or USIM card on the tray with the gold-colored contacts facing upwards and gently press the SIM or USIM card into the tray to make it firm.

4   Carefully insert the tray back into the tray slot.

CAUTION:

- Press the ejection pin into the **tray's hole** to expose the tray.

- Use only a nano-SIM card.

- Be cautious not to lose your SIM or USIM card, or allow others have unauthorized access to it. Samsung does not accept any legal responsibility for any damages or inconveniences experience as a result of lost or stolen cards.

- Check to ascertain hat the ejection pin is perpendicular to the hole. Or else, the device may be damaged.

- If you do not fix the SIM card firmly into the tray, it may fall out of the tray unawares.

- If you insert a wet tray into your device, your device may get damaged. Always make sure the tray is dry before inserting it into your device.

- Ensure the tray is completely inserted into the tray slot to prevent liquid from entering your device.

How to correctly install SIM card (dual SIM card tray)

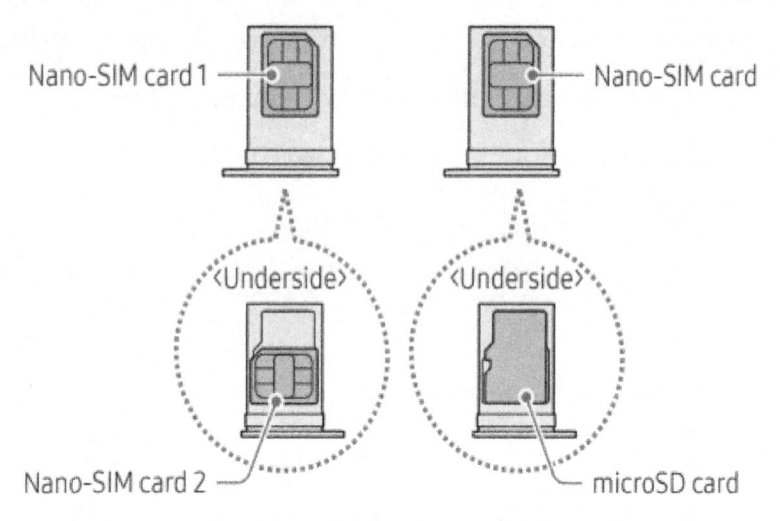

Nano-SIM card 1

Nano-SIM card

⟨Underside⟩

⟨Underside⟩

Nano-SIM card 2

microSD card

How to activate an eSIM on your Galaxy A55 5G

Head To the **Settings** menu and tap **Connections**, select **SIM manager**, and then, **Add eSIM**. Find a suitable mobile plan and activate the eSIM following the on-screen prompts.

If your carrier provided a QR code, go to **Settings**, tap **Connections**, tap **SIM manager**, then **Add eSIM**, and then select **Scan QR code from service provider**, and lastly, scan the QR code.

SIM card manager (dual SIM models)

Open the **Settings** app, then tap **Connections**, and tap **SIM card manager**.

- **SIM cards**: Activate the SIM card to start using it and customize the SIM card settings.
- **eSIMs**: Activate the embedded SIM (eSIM)
- **Preferred SIM card**: Choose which specific SIM cards you would want to use for some features, such as voice calls, when two cards are activated.
- **Auto data switching:** If the device's primary SIM card can't connect to the network, set it to use another SIM card for data services.
- **More SIM card settings**: Change and personalize the call settings.

How to insert an SD card

The maximum capacity of the SD card your device can hold may differ from other models'. Some SD cards may have incompatibility issues with your smartphone, depending on the manufacturer and type of the SD card. To know your device's SD memory card capacity, please visit the Samsung website.

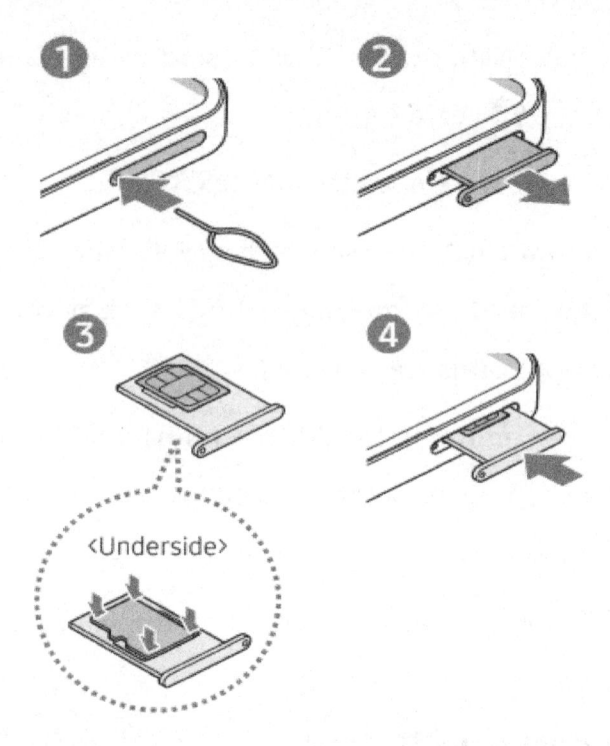

1. Safely insert the ejection pin into the hole on the tray to release the tray.
2. Pull out the tray from the tray slot with caution.
3. Put a memory card on the tray with the gold-colored contacts facing upwards and gently press the memory card into the tray to make it firm.
4. Insert the tray back into the tray slot carefully.

CAUTION:

- Press the ejection pin into the **tray's hole** to expose the tray.

- Some memory cards may not be wholly compatible with the device. Using a memory card that is not compatible with your device result in damage to the device or the memory card, or corrupt the data you have stored in them.
- Carefully insert the memory card right-side up.
- Confirm that the ejection pin is perpendicular to the hole. Or else, the device may get damaged.
- Removing the tray from the device disables the mobile data connection.
- If you don't fix the card firmly into the tray, the memory card may leave or fall out of the tray.
- If you insert a wet tray into your device, the device may be damaged. Always make sure the tray is dry before insert it into your device.
- Be cautious to insert the tray completely into the tray slot to avoid liquid from entering your device.

NOTE:
- The device complies with the FAT and the exFAT file systems for SD cards. When you insert an SD card that has been formatted in a different file system into your device, it will request you to format the card

again in your device or else, it will not identify the card. To use the SD card, you must first of all format it. If your device cannot format or identify the memory card, contact the SD card manufacturer or a Samsung Service Centre.

- Frequent writing and erasing of data reduce the lifespan of memory cards.

- When inserting an SD card into your smartphone, you'll see the SD card's file directory in the **My Files** > **SD card** folder.

How to safely remove an SD card from your Galaxy A55 5G

Before you take out the SD card, you must first unmount it. Open the **Settings** app and tap **Device care**, then select **Storage**. Swipe to the left to display the **SD card** page. Then tap **More options ⋮** and tap **Unmount**.

CAUTION: Never remove external storage, such as a memory card or USB storage, while the device is transferring or accessing information, or right after transferring data. Doing so may lead to data corruption or loss or cause damage to the external storage or device. Samsung is not responsible for losses, including data loss, that happen when external storage devices are used in the wrong way.

Formatting the microSD card

A microSD card that has been formatted on a computer may not be compatible with the device. It is recommended that you format the SD card on the device.

Open the **Settings** app and tap **Device care** > **Storage**. Swipe to the left to display the **SD card** page, tap **More options ⋮** and then tap **Format**.

CAUTION: Before you format the memory card, remember to make backup copies of all important data stored in the memory card. Loss of data resulting from user actions is not covered in the manufacturer's warranty.

How to turn on and off the Galaxy A55 5G

To turn on your device, simply **press and hold the Side button for a few seconds**.

When it comes to turning off your phone, there are several ways to do that. Below are four methods you can use to power off your Galaxy A55 5G phone.

1. Press and hold the **Side button** and the **Volume Down button** simultaneously for a few seconds. The Power menu will appear on the screen. Tap the **Power off** option.

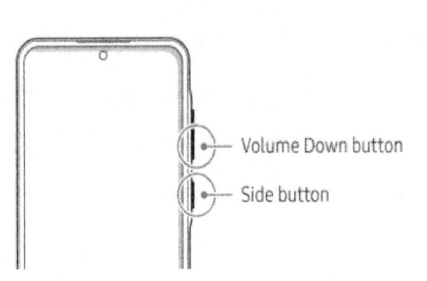

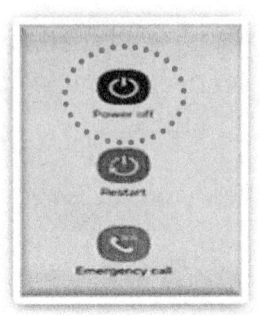

2. Alternatively, swipe down twice from the top of the screen, tap the Power off icon ⏻ at the top right corner of the screen to bring up the Power menu, and then tap the **Power off** option.

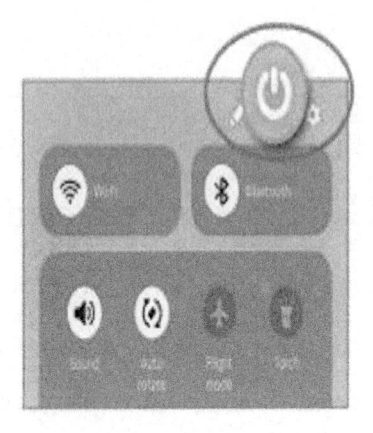

3. Set the **Side button** to turn off the device when you press and hold the button. Simply go to **Settings**, scroll down and select **Advanced features,** select **Side button,** and then select the **Power off menu** option under the **Press and hold** section.

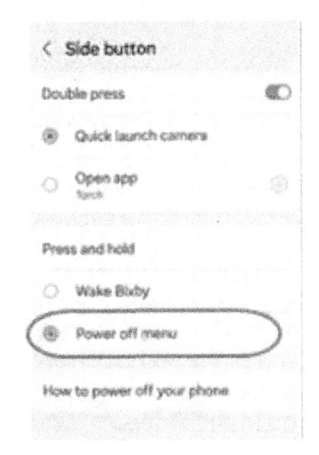

4. The last option is to ask **Bixby** to turn off the phone for you.

NOTE: If you want to restart the device, tap **Restart** when the power menu appears on the screen.

Forcing restart

If your device becomes frozen and unresponsive, press and hold the Side key and the Volume Down key simultaneously for a period longer than 7 seconds to restart it.

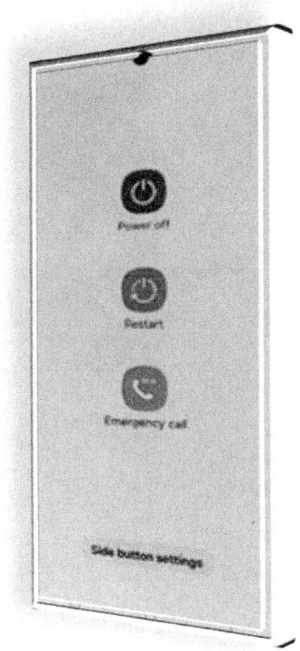

Emergency mode

You may switch the device to emergency mode to reduce battery consumption. Some apps and functions will be limited. In emergency mode, you can make an emergency call, send your current location information to others, sound an emergency alarm, etc. with your device.

To activate the Emergency mode in your device, press and hold the Side key and the Volume Down key simultaneously, then tap **Emergency call**. Alternatively, you can open the notification panel, swipe downwards, tap ⏻, and then tap **Emergency call**.

CHAPTER 2:
SETTING UP YOUR DEVICE

Initial setup

When you turn on your Galaxy phone for the first time or after performing a data reset, make sure to follow the on-screen instructions to set up your device.

NOTE: Unless you connect to a Wi-Fi network, you may not be able to set up some device features during the initial setup.

How to set up Samsung account on your Galaxy A55 5G

Your Samsung account is an integrated account service that lets you use several of Samsung services offered on mobile devices, TVs, and the Samsung website.

To see the list of services that can be used with your Samsung account, please visit account.samsung.com.

1. Go to the **Settings** app, tap **Accounts and backup** > **Manage accounts** > **Add account** > **Samsung account**.

    Alternatively, open the **Settings** menu and tap **Samsung account**.

2. If you already have an existing Samsung account, sign in to your account. If not, tap "**Forgot password or don't have an account?**", and then tap **Create account** to sign up for a Samsung account,

How to Find your ID and reset your password

If you ever forget your Samsung account ID or password, tap "**Forgot password or don't have an account?**", select either **Forgot ID** (to find your ID) or **Forgot password** (to reset your password) on the Samsung account sign-in screen. Although you'll need to provide some important information before you can successfully recover your ID or reset your password.

Signing out of your Samsung account

Any time you sign out of your Samsung account, your data, such as contacts or events, will also be removed from your device.

1. From your **Settings** menu, tap **Accounts and back-up**, then **Manage accounts**.
2. Tap **Samsung** account, then go to **My profile** and tap **Sign out** which can be found at the bottom of the screen.
3. Tap **Sign out**, then input your Samsung account password, and tap **OK**.

Transferring data from your previous device to your new Galaxy A55 5G(Smart Switch)

You can use Smart Switch to transfer data from your old device to your new device. Open the **Settings** app and tap **Accounts and backup > Bring data from old device**.
NOTE:

- This feature may not be available on some devices or computers.
- Restrictions apply. Please visit www.samsung.com/smartswitch for details. Samsung takes copyright as sacrosanct. You should only transfer content that you own or have the right to transfer.

Transferring data using a USB cable

You can connect your old device to your device with the USB cable to effortlessly and quickly transfer data.

1 Connect your new Galaxy A55 5G phone and the previous device using your phone's USB cable. A USB connector may be needed depending on your old device.

2 When the app selection pop-up window displays, tap **Smart Switch > Receive data**.

3 On your old device, tap **Connect**.

If you do not have the app, download it from **Galaxy Store** or **Play Store**.

Your device will automatically recognize the previous device and display a list of data you can transfer.

4 On your Galaxy A55 5G phone, choose an item to bring and tap **Next** and follow the onscreen instructions to complete transferring the data.

CAUTION: Never disconnect the USB cable from the device when you are transferring files. Doing so may cause data loss or damage your device.

NOTE: Transferring data increases the rate of battery power consumption by your device. Make sure your device is well charged before transferring data. Low battery power may cause interruption of data transfer.

How to Transfer your data wirelessly

Transfer data from your previous device to your new Galaxy A55 5G wirelessly via Wi-Fi Direct by following the simple steps:

1 Launch the **Smart Switch** app on your old device.

If you do not have the app in the device, download it from **Galaxy Store** or **Play Store**.

2. On your new phone, open the **Settings** app and tap **Accounts and backup** > **Transfer data for device setup**.
3. Place the devices close to each other.
4. On your old device, tap **Send data** > **Wireless**.
5. On your new phone, tap **Receive data**. Select the operating system (Android, iOS or Windows) of your old device and tap **Wireless**.

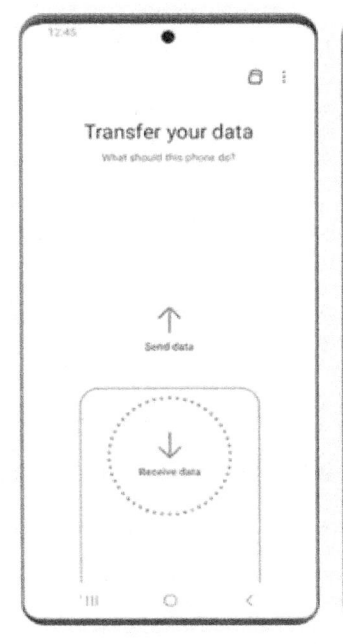

6. On your old device, tap **Connect**.
7. On your new Galaxy A55 phone, select an option and tap **Next**. Follow the onscreen commands to complete transferring data.

How to use external storage to backup and restore data

Transfer data using external storage, such as a microSD (memory) card.

1. Back up data from your old device to external storage.
2. Insert or make a connection between the external storage device and your smartphone.
3. On your smartphone, go to the **Settings** app and tap **Accounts and backup > External storage transfer**.
4. Choose the backup data under **Restore from** and tap **Next**.
5. Follow the on-screen instructions to transfer data from external storage.

Transferring backup data from a computer to your new Galaxy A55 5G

You can transfer the data you've backed up on a computer from your old device to your new smartphone. However, you must first of all download the Smart Switch computer version app from www.samsung.com/smartswitch. To do this, follow these simple steps:

1. Go to www.samsung.com/smartswitch on your computer to download **Smart Switch**.

2. On the computer, launch the **Smart Switch** app.

   NOTE: If your previous device is not a Samsung device, then you've got to back up your data to a computer using a program provided by the device's manufacturer. Then, skip to the fifth step.

3. Now, connect your previous device to the computer using the device's USB cable.

4. Following the on-screen instructions on the computer, back up data from the device.

5. Thereafter, disconnect your previous device from the computer.

6. Now, connect your new Galaxy A55 phone to the computer using the USB cable.

7. On the computer, follow the on-screen instructions in order to transfer data to your new device.

Face recognition

You can set the device to unlock the screen by merely recognizing your face.

NOTE:

- If you use your face as a screen lock method, your face cannot be used to unlock the screen for the first time you turn on the device. To use the device, you must first of all unlock the screen using the pattern, PIN, or password that you set when registering the face. Be cautious not to forget your pattern, PIN, or password.

- If you change the screen lock method to **Swipe** or **None**, which are not safe methods, all of your biometric data will be removed. If you choose to use your biometric data in apps or features, you must re-register your biometric data.

Precautions for using face recognition

Before using the face recognition to unlock your device, remember the following precautions:

- Someone or something else that looks like your image could be able to unlock your device.

- Face recognition is not as secure as Pattern, PIN, or Password.

Tips for better face recognition

Consider the following when using face recognition:
- Consider the circumstances under which you're registering, such as wearing glasses, hats, masks, beards, or heavy makeup
- Make sure you're in a well-lit area and that the camera lens is clean when registering
- Be sure your image is not blurry for better match results

How to register your face

For a more accurate face registration, register your face indoors and avoid direct sunlight.

1. From the Settings screen, click **Security and privacy**, select **Biometrics,** and then select **Face recognition**.
2. Read the on-screen instructions and click **Continue**.
3. Set your preferred screen lock method.
4. Position your face inside the frame on the screen to enable the camera to scan your face.

NOTE:
- If unlocking the screen with your face is not working appropriately, click **Remove face data** to re-

move your registered face and register your face again.

- To improve the face recognition, click the option that says "**Add alternative appearance to enhance recognition**" and add an alternate appearance.

How to unlock the screen with your face

You can use your face to unlock the device's screen instead of using a pattern, PIN, or password.

1. Go to the Settings screen, click **Security and Privacy,** select **Biometrics,** and the select **Face recognition**.
2. Unlock the screen by simply using the preset screen lock method.
3. Click the **Face unlock** switch to activate the feature.
4. On the locked screen, look directly at the screen.

   If it recognizes your face, you can unlock the screen without using any extra screen lock method. If your face is not recognized, then you have to use the preset screen lock method.

How to delete the registered face data

You can remove face data that you have registered.

1. Go to the Settings screen, click **Security and Privacy,** select **Biometrics,** and the select **Face recognition.**
2. Unlock the screen by simply using the preset screen lock method.
3. Click **Remove face data → Remove.**

   As soon as the registered face is deleted, all the related features will also be deactivated.

Fingerprint recognition

Before you can use fingerprint recognition, you must first register and save your fingerprint information in your device.

NOTE:

- Availability of this feature depends on the service provider or model.
- Fingerprint recognition uses the unique characteristics of each fingerprint to increase the security of your device. The likelihood of the fingerprint sensor confusing two different fingerprints is very minimal. Nevertheless, in rare occasions where separate finger-

prints are very similar, the sensor may recognize them as alike.

- If you use a screen protector, ensure it permits for use of the On-screen fingerprint sensor.
- If you use your fingerprint as a screen lock method, you will not be able to use it to unlock the screen for the first time after turning on the device. To use the device, you must first of all unlock the screen using the pattern, PIN, or password you set during the registration of the fingerprint. Be cautious not to forget your pattern, PIN, or password.
- If the device does not recognize your fingerprint, unlock the device using the pattern, PIN, or password you set during the registration of the fingerprint, and then register your fingerprints again. If you forget your pattern, PIN, or password, you will not be able to use the device unless you reset it. Samsung is not accountable for any loss of data or inconvenience that may be caused by forgotten unlock codes.
- If you change the screen lock method to **Swipe** or **None**, which do not give adequate security, all of your biometric data will be deleted from the device. If

you want to use your biometric data in apps or features, you must first re-register your biometric data.

Tips for better fingerprint recognition

When you scan your fingerprints on the device, be conscious of the following conditions that may affect the feature's performance:

- The device may not be able to recognize fingerprints if they are affected by wrinkles or scars.
- The device may not recognize fingerprints from fingers that are too small or thin.
- In order to improve recognition performance, register fingerprints of the hand that is most often used to operate the device.
- There is a built-in fingerprint recognition sensor at the bottom center of your device's screen. Make sure that you secure the screen protector or the touch screen on the fingerprint recognition sensor area from scratches or damages by objects, such as coins, keys, pens, and necklaces.
- Make sure that the fingerprint recognition sensor area right at the bottom center of the screen and your fingers are clean and dry when fingerprinting.

- If your finger is not placed properly on the surface of the fingerprint recognition area, the device may not recognize your fingerprints. Avoid bending your finger or using a fingertip. Press the screen tightly with your finger in a way that your fingertip spreads over the wide surface of the fingerprint recognition area.

How to register your fingerprints

1. Navigate to the Settings screen, click **Security and Privacy,** select **Biometrics,** and then select **Fingerprints.**
2. Read the on-screen instructions and click **Continue.**
3. Set a preferred screen lock method.
4. Click **Register** and Position your finger on the fingerprint recognition sensor. When the device detects your finger, pull it up and place it on the fingerprint recognition sensor again.

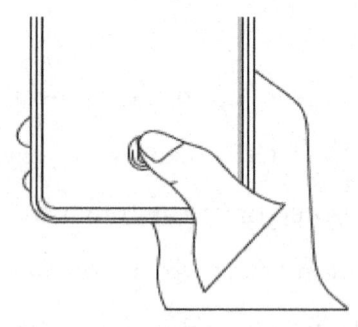

Repeat the process until the fingerprint is registered.

5   When you are through registering your fingerprints, click **Done**.

You can check whether your fingerprint is registered by clicking **Check added fingerprints**.

Unlocking the screen with your fingerprints

You can unlock the screen with your fingerprint if you do not want to use a pattern, PIN, or password.

1   Navigate to the Settings screen, click **Security and Privacy,** select **Biometrics,** and the select **Fingerprints**.

2   Unlock the screen by using the current screen lock method.

3   Press the **Fingerprint unlock** switch to turn it on.

4   On the locked screen, put your finger on the fingerprint recognition sensor and scan your fingerprint.

Changing the fingerprint recognition icon setting

Set the device to display or hide the fingerprint recognition icon when you click the screen while the screen is turned off.

1   From the Settings screen, click **Security and privacy > Biometrics > Fingerprints**.

2   Unlock the screen by using the current screen lock technique.

3   Click **Show icon when screen is off** and choose an option.

Deleting registered fingerprints

You can delete registered fingerprints.

1   From the Settings screen, click **Security and privacy > Biometrics > Fingerprints**.

2   Unlock the screen by using the current method of screen lock.

3   Select a fingerprint to delete and click **Remove**.

Samsung Pay

Register cards to Samsung Pay to make online and offline payments easily and safely.

You can get additional information, such as cards that support this feature at www.samsung.com/samsung-pay.

NOTE:

- To make payments with Samsung Pay, you may be required to connect the device to a Wi-Fi or mobile network depending on the region.

- Availability of this feature is dependent on the service provider or model.

- The procedures for the initial setup and card registration may not be the same, depending on the service provider or model.

How to Set up Samsung Pay on your Galaxy A55 5G Smartphone

If you're running this app for the first time or restarting it after performing a data reset, follow the instructions displayed on the screen to complete the initial setup.

1. Open the **Samsung Pay** app.
2. Sign in to your Samsung account, then read and agree to the terms and conditions.
3. Register your fingerprint as well as a PIN to use when making payments.

    This PIN is going to be used to verify several actions in Samsung Pay, such as making payments and unlocking the app.

Registering cards

Samsung Pay is linked with some of the most reputable financial institutions and credit card companies in the United States, like American Express, Visa, and MasterCard, so you're rest assured of seamless payment options, whether in-person, online or in an app on your phone.

Open the **Samsung Pay** app and follow the on-screen instructions to finish your card registration.

1. Find the Samsung Pay app and launch it on your mobile device.
2. Tap the **Menu** button (those three horizontal lines) in the upper left corner of the screen, and then select **Cards** from the menu that appears.

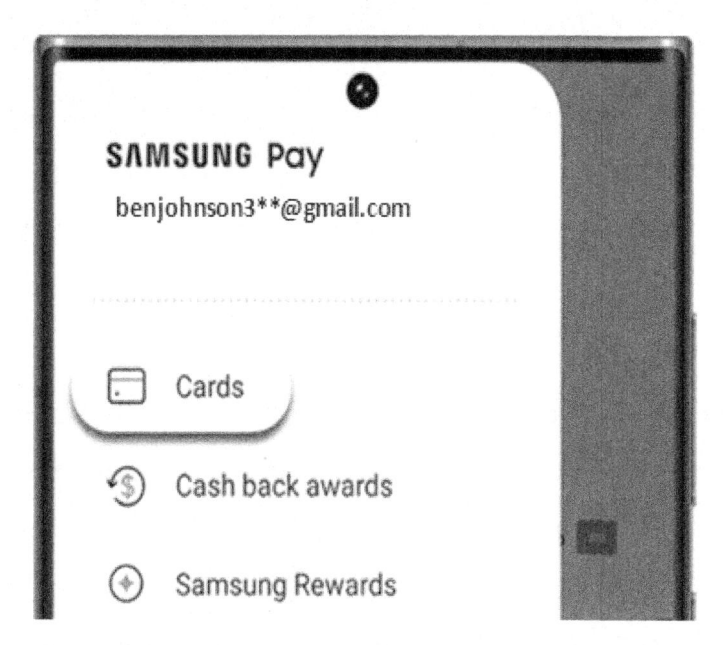

> **SAMSUNG Pay**
>
> benjohnson3**@gmail.com
>
> ▢ Cards
>
> ⑤ Cash back awards
>
> ⊕ Samsung Rewards

3. Then, select the **Add card** icon, which resembles a credit card and has a plus sign placed next to it. Then, click **Add credit/debit card**.
4. To register your card, just follow the on-screen instructions. When you add a card, you are required to agree to the terms and conditions associated with that card.
5. Please get in touch with the card issuer if you have any issues regarding the conditions.
6. After the card has been added, you will be able to begin using it to make purchases using your phone in stores immediately!

7. **Take note** that you have the ability to add and manage up to ten different payment cards, including both debit and credit cards. You also have the option of adding an unlimited number of gift cards to your account.

How to manage your cards

Why not add a card to your Favorite Cards collection if you find that you use that particular card more frequently than others? You can do all of this and more by going into the card's settings.

Launch **Samsung Pay** app on your mobile device. Then, select **Menu** (the three lines in the upper-left corner), then select **Cards**. You may then choose the payment card of your choice from there. You have access to the following choices when you are in this screen:

- To add or delete a card from your Favorite Cards, tap the **More options** button (it looks like three vertical dots). You also have the option of deleting the card from Samsung Pay anytime you wish.

- Tap the **Info** icon to discover the card issuer's customer support number or to download their mobile app (it looks like the letter "i").

- Swipe up from the bottom of the screen to see the most recent transactions that have been made using the card.

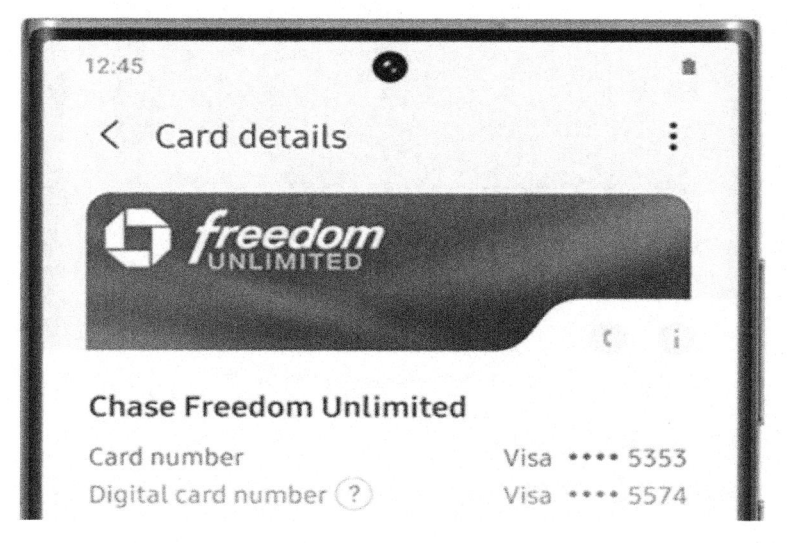

![Card details screen showing Chase Freedom Unlimited with Visa ••••5353 and Visa ••••5574]

How to view the last four-digit number of your cards

The digital number on your card can be required if you are making a return at a store. You can easily locate this information inside Samsung Pay in order to provide it to the cashier when they ask for it.

Launch **Samsung Pay** on your mobile device. Then, select **Menu** (the three lines in the top left corner), then select **Cards**. After that, choose the card that you want. You'll see last four digits of the digital card number shown next to the phrase "**Digital card number**."

When you access your **Favorite Cards** in Samsung Pay, you will also be able to view the digital card number associated with the card. Next to each card that appears on the page that lists your Favorite Cards will be the digital card number.

How to delete card from your Samsung pay

If there is a card in your Samsung Pay account that you don't actually use anymore, you have the ability to delete it whenever you want. But, keep in mind that even after you remove a card from Samsung Pay, the card itself will continue to function normally. Get in touch with the company that issued your card if you'd like to cancel it.

Step 1: launch the **Samsung Pay** app on your mobile device, tap the **Menu** button (the three horizontal lines), and then select **Cards**.

Step 2: choose the card you want to get rid of and tap "**More options**" (the three vertical dots).

Step 3: Tap **Delete card**. It is likely that you will be prompted to enter your Samsung Pay PIN or to authenticate using biometrics.

45

Making payments

1 Click and hold a card image at the bottom of the screen and pull it upwards. You can also open the **Samsung Pay** app, then on the cards list, swipe to the left or right and choose a card to use.

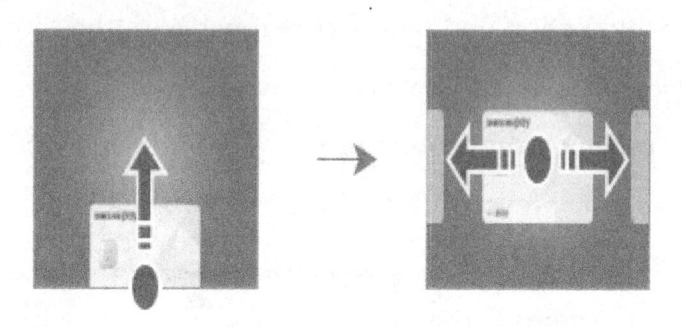

2 Scan your fingerprint or input the payment PIN you set.

3 Touch the back of your device to feel the card reader. Once the card reader is able to recognize the card information, the payment will be processed.

NOTE:

- The processing of payments may be affected by your network connection.
- The verification method for payments may not be the same, depending on the card readers.

Cancelling payments

You can cancel payments by visiting the place where you made the transactions.

On the cards list, swipe to the left or right to pick the card you used. Follow the on-screen instructions to complete the cancellation of your payments.

Samsung Pass

Register your biometric data to Samsung Pass and easily verify your identity when using services which have need of your login or personal information.

NOTE:

- You can use the website sign-in feature only for websites that you access via the **Internet** app. Some websites may not support this feature.
- Registered biometric data is saved to your device alone. It is not synced with other devices or servers.

Registering Samsung Pass

Before using Samsung Pass, you have to register your biometric data to Samsung Pass.

On the Settings screen, click **Security and privacy** > **More security settings** > **Samsung Pass**. Complete the setup by following the on-screen instructions.

Verifying the Samsung account password

You can use your registered biometric data to confirm your identity instead of using your Samsung account password wherever necessary, e.g. when you purchase content from **Galaxy Store**.

On the Samsung Pass main screen, click ⋮ → **Settings** → **Account and syncing**, and then click the **Verify with Samsung Pass** switch to activate it.

Using Samsung Pass to sign in to websites

Samsung Pass can be used to easily sign in to websites that support ID and password autofill.

1   On the sign-in page of the website, input your ID and password, and then click the website's sign-in button.

2   When a pop-up window asking whether you want to save the sign-in information displays, mark **Sign in with Samsung Pass** and click **Remember**.

Using Samsung Pass to sign in to apps

Samsung Pass can be used to easily sign in to apps that support ID and password autofill.

1   On the sign-in page of the app, input your ID and password, and then click the app's sign-in button.

2   When a pop-up window asking whether you want to save the sign-in information displays, click **Save**.

Managing sign-in information

Take a look the list of websites and apps you have set to use Samsung Pass and manage information about your sign-in.

1   On the Samsung Pass main screen, click **Apps** or **Websites** and choose a website or app from the list.

2   Click **Edit** and change your ID, password, and the website's or app's name.

To delete your sign-in information, click **Delete**.

Using Samsung Pass with websites and apps

If you're using websites or apps that support Samsung Pass, you can easily sign in with Samsung Pass.

To know if a website and app supports Samsung Pass, on the Samsung Pass main screen, click ⋮ → **Partners**. If there are no websites or apps that support Samsung Pass, you will not see **Partners**.

Entering your personal information automatically

Your Samsung Pass can be used to easily enter your personal information, such as your address or payment card information, on apps that support autofill.

1   On the Samsung Pass main screen, choose an option under **Private info**.

2   Enter the information and click **Save**.

You can now use the biometric data you registered to Samsung Pass when entering the personal information automatically on apps that support this feature.

Deleting your Samsung Pass data

You can be able delete your biometric data, sign-in information, and app data registered to Samsung Pass.

From the Samsung Pass main screen, click ⋮→ **Settings** → **See all devices using Samsung Pass**→⋮→**Leave Samsung Pass**.

NOTE:

- Your Samsung account will remain active.
- The Samsung Pass data on other devices signed in to your Samsung account will also be deleted.

How to install or uninstall apps on your new Galaxy A55 5G

Galaxy Store

Buy and download apps. You can download apps that are tailored to Samsung Galaxy devices.

Launch the **Galaxy Store** app. Surf apps by category or tap the **Search** icon Q to search for keywords.

NOTE:

- This app may not be present depending on the service provider or model.
- To modify the auto update settings, tap **Menu,** tap the **Settings cog** ⚙ and then tap **Auto update apps**, and then select an option.

Play Store

Buy and download apps.

Launch the **Play Store** app. Surf apps by category or search for apps by keyword.

NOTE: To modify the auto update settings, tap the icon for your account, the go to **Settings** > **Network Preferences** > **Auto-update apps**, and then pick from the available options.

Managing apps

Uninstalling or disabling apps

Tap and hold an app and select from the options:

- **Uninstall**: Uninstall downloaded apps.
- **Disable**: Disable marked default apps that cannot be uninstalled from the device.

NOTE: Some apps may not function with this feature.

Enabling apps

Launch the **Settings** app, tap **Apps** > ▤ > **Disabled** > **OK**, choose the app you want, and then tap **Enable**.

How to set app permissions

For some apps to function well, they may request permission to access or use information on your device.

To see your app permission settings, launch the **Settings** app and tap **Apps**. Pick an app and tap **Permissions**. You can peruse the app's permissions list and change its permissions.

To display or modify app permission settings by permission category, launch the **Settings** app and tap **Apps** > ⋮ > **Permission manager**. Pick an item and then an app.

NOTE: Unless you grant permissions to apps, the basic features of the apps may not work optimally.

CHAPTER 3

BASIC FEATURES AND FUNCTIONS

Understanding the screen

Controlling the touch screen

Tapping
Tap the screen.

Tapping and holding
Tap and hold the screen for approximately 2 seconds.

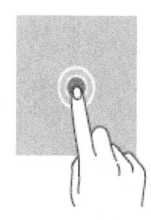

Dragging
Tap and hold an item and drag it to the target position.

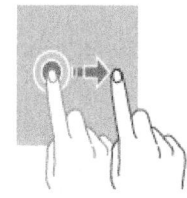

Double-tapping
Double-tap the screen.

Swiping
Swipe upwards, downwards, to the left, or to the right.

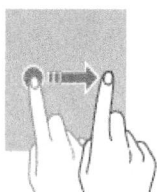

Spreading and pinching
Spread two fingers apart or pinch on the screen.

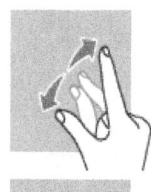

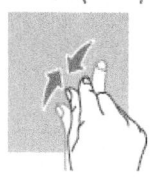

CAUTION:

- Never allow the touch screen to come into contact with other electrical devices. Electrostatic discharges can make the touch screen to malfunction.

- To avoid damaging the touch screen, do not tap it with anything sharp object, or apply any excessive pressure to it with your fingertips.

- It is recommended not to use fixed graphics on part or all of the touch screen for prolonged periods as this may cause afterimages (screen burn-in) or ghosting.

NOTE:

The device may not be able to identify touch inputs close to the edges of the screen, which are not within the touch input area.

Navigation bar (soft buttons)

Any time you turn on the screen, the soft buttons will display on the navigation bar at the bottom of the screen. By default, the soft buttons are configured to the **Recents** button, **Home** button, and **Back** button from left to right respectively. The functions of the buttons can change depending on the app currently being used or operating environment. (See *Soft buttons and their functions* in Chapter One for more information).

Hiding the navigation bar

Hiding the navigation bar enables you to view files or use apps on a wider screen.

From the **Settings** app, tap **Display** > **Navigation bar**, and then tap **Swipe gestures** under **Navigation type**. The navigation bar will be hidden and the gesture hints will show up. Tap **More options** and select your desired option.

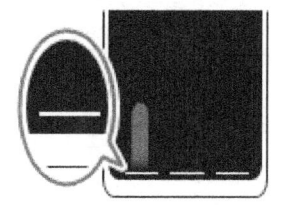

Swipe from bottom   Swipe from sides and bottom

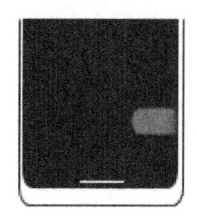

If you like to hide the gesture hints at the bottom of the screen, tap the **Gesture hints** switch to deactivate it.

Home screen and Apps screen

The Home screen is the starting point from where you can access all of the features of your device. It shows widgets, shortcuts to apps, and much more.

The Apps screen displays icons for all apps installed on your device.

How to switch quickly between Home and Apps screens

To open the Apps screen, swipe the Home screen upwards. To return to the Home screen, swipe the Apps screen upwards or downwards; or instead, tap the Home button or the Back button.

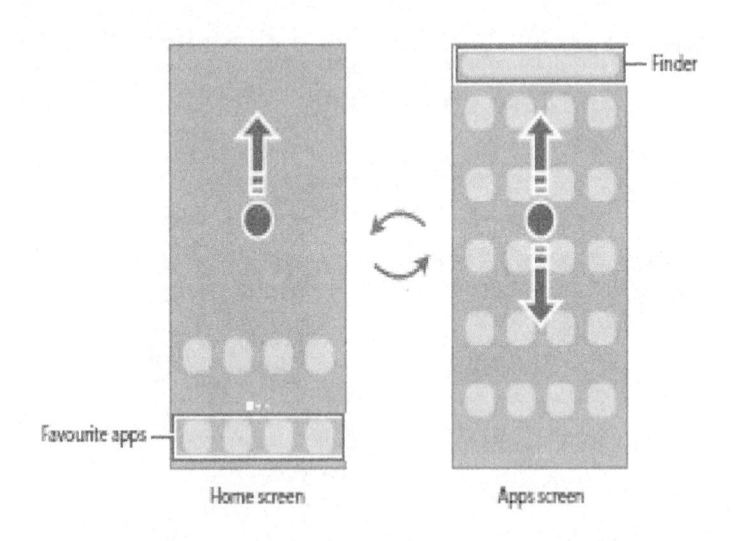

If the Apps button has been added on the Home screen, you can open the Apps screen simply by tapping the button. To add it, follow the simple steps:

1. On the Home screen, tap and hold an empty area.
2. Tap **Settings**
3. Activate the **Show Apps screen button on Home screen** by tapping the switch.

The Apps button is straightaway added at the bottom of the Home screen.

How to make edits on the Home screen

From the Home screen, **tap and hold an empty area, or pinch your fingers together to view the editing options**. Here, you can set the wallpaper; add widgets; and add, delete, or rearrange Home screen panels.

- To add panels, swipe to the left, and then tap ⊕.
- To move panels, tap and hold a panel preview, then drag it to a new location.
- To delete panels, tap the bin icon 🗑 on the panel.

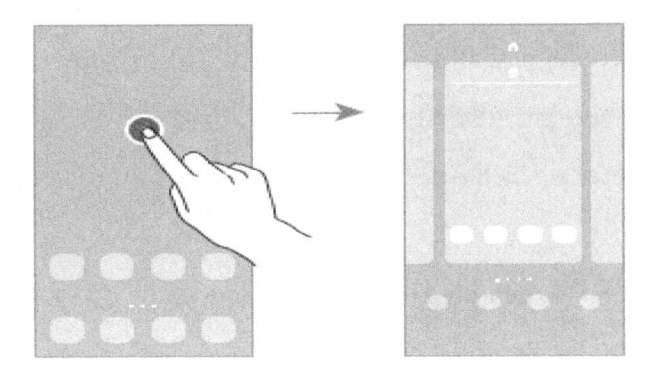

- **Wallpapers and style**: You can change the wallpaper settings for the Home screen and the locked screen.

- **Themes**: You can change the device's theme. Note that visual elements of interface, such as colors, icons, and wallpapers, will change according to the selected theme.

- **Widgets**: These are small apps that launch specific app functions to give information and convenient access on your Home screen. Select a widget and tap **Add**. The widget will be added on the Home screen accordingly.

- **Settings**: Organize settings for the Home screen, such as the screen layout.

Displaying all apps on the Home screen

If you don't want to use a separate Apps screen, you can set the device to display all your apps on the Home screen. On the Home screen, just tap and hold an empty area, and then tap **Settings** > **Home screen layout** > **Home screen only** > **Apply**.

With that, you'll be able to access all your apps by swiping to the left on the Home screen.

Launching Finder

Quickly search for content on the device.

1. On the Apps screen, tap **Search**. Otherwise, open the notification panel and swipe downwards, then tap 🔍.
2. Type in a keyword. All the apps and content on your device will be searched.

You can search for more content by taping 🔍 on the keyboard.

Moving items

1. Tap and hold an item
2. Drag it to a new location.
3. Drag it to the side of the screen if you want to move the item to another panel.

Adding a shortcut to an app on the Home screen:

1. Tap and hold an item on the Apps screen
2. Tap **Add to Home**.

If you like, you can also move frequently used apps to the shortcuts area at the bottom of the Home screen.

Creating folders

Create folders and collect related apps to quickly access and launch apps.

1. On the Home screen or the Apps screen, tap and hold an app

2. Drag the selected app over another app. A new folder comprising the selected apps will be created. 3. Tap **Folder name** and input a folder name.

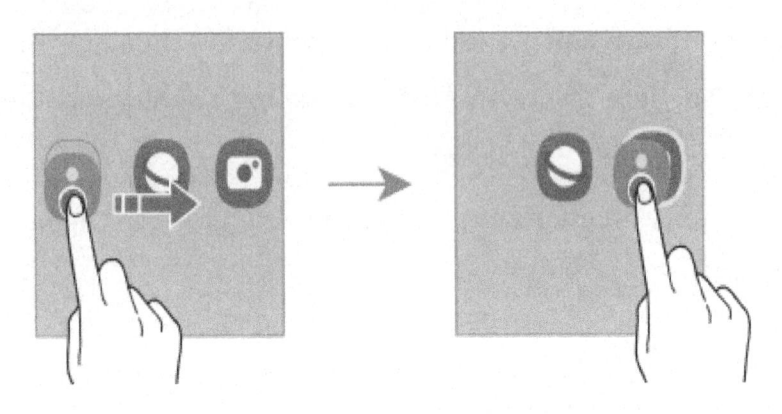

- **Adding more apps**

    Simply tap ➕ on the folder. Select the apps to add by ticking them and tap **Done**. Alternately, just drag the app you want to add to the folder.

- **Moving apps from a folder**

    Tap and hold an app if you want to drag it to a new location.

- **Deleting a folder**

    Tap and hold a folder, and then tap the **Delete folder**. Note that only the folder will be deleted. The apps in the folder will be relocated to the Apps screen.

Edge panel

The Edge panel enables you to quickly access your favorite apps and features.

Pull the Edge panel handle towards the center of the screen.

If the Edge panel handle is not visible on the screen, go to the **Settings** app, tap **Display**, and then tap the **Edge panels** switch to activate.

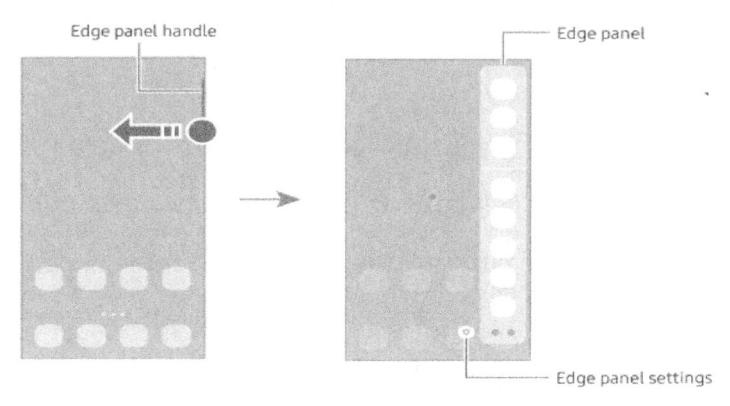

Lock screen

Whenever you press the Side key, you'll make the screen to turn off and lock. The screen will also turn off and automatically lock if the device is not used for a given period.

To unlock the screen, turn it on and swipe in any direction of the screen.

If the screen is off, press the Side key to turn it on or you double-click the screen.

Changing the screen lock method

To modify how the screen locks, launch the **Settings** app, tap **Lock screen** > **Screen lock type**, and then choose a method.

Setting a pattern, PIN, password, or your biometric data for the screen lock method protects your personal information by preventing others from having unauthorized access to your device. After setting the screen lock method, the device will require an unlock code anytime you want to unlock it.

NOTE: If you want your device to do a factory data reset if you enter the unlock code wrong too many times in a row and reach the maximum number of attempts, open the **Settings** app, click **Lock screen** > **Secure lock settings**, unlock the screen using the preset screen lock method, and then tap the **Auto factory reset** switch to turn it on.

Indicator icons

Indicator icons will show on the status bar at the top of the screen. The icons shown in the table below are most commonly in use:

Icon	Meaning
⊘	No signal
▁▃▅	Signal strength
ᴿ▁▃▅	Roaming (outside of normal service area)
G ↓↑	GPRS network connected
E ↓↑	EDGE network connected
3G ↓↑	UMTS network connected
H ↓↑	HSDPA network connected
H+ ↓↑	HSPA+ network connected
4G ↓↑ / LTE ↓↑	LTE network connected
5G ↓↑	5G network connected
5G ↓↑	Connected to LTE network with the 5G network
📶	Wi-Fi connected
✳	Bluetooth feature activated
◉	Location services being used
☎	Call in progress
☏	Missed call
💬	New text or multimedia message
⏰	Alarm activated

63

🔇 / 📳	Mute mode / Vibration mode
✈	Flight mode activated
⚠	Error occurred or caution required
/ 🔋 🔋	Battery charging / Battery power level

NOTE:

- The status bar may not show at the top of the screen in some apps. To show the status bar, drag down from the top of the screen.

- Some indicator icons show only when you open the notification panel.

- The indicator icons may show separately based on the service provider or model.

Notification panel

Anytime you receive new notifications, indicator icons will show on the status bar. To see additional information about the icons, open the notification panel and view the details.

Quick settings — Open **Settings**.

Control connected nearby devices and SmartThings devices and scenes.

Adjust the brightness of the display.

Control media on your phone and connected nearby devices.

Check the notification details and perform various actions.

Clear all notifications.

Access the notification settings.

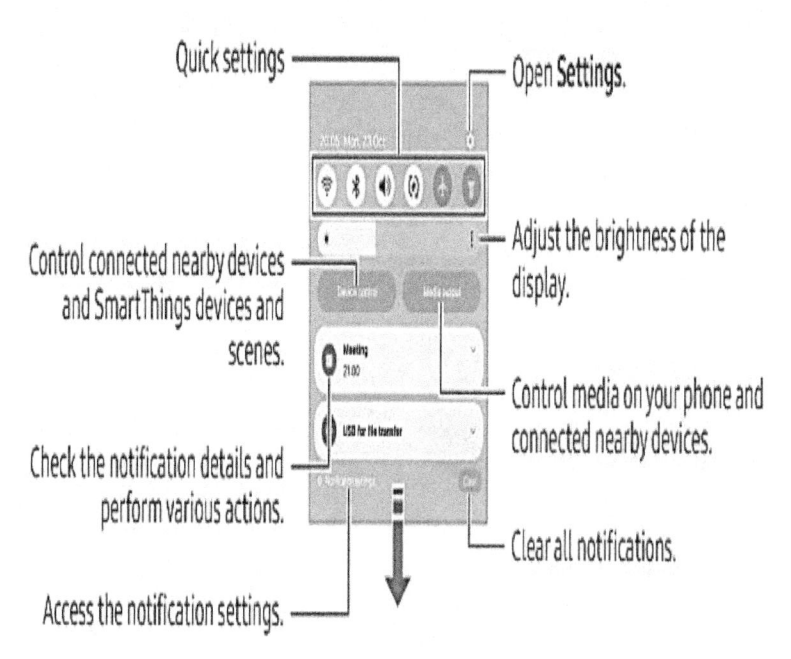

Drag the status bar downwards to open the notification panel, and swipe upwards on the screen to close it.

The following functions on the notification panel commonly used:

Using quick setting buttons

Simply swipe downwards on the notification panel or swipe down twice from the top of the screen on the Home screen to open the Quick settings panel. Tap any button to activate its specific features. Touch and hold any button or simply tap its name to get additional settings. Tap ✐ at the top of the screen and select **Edit** to make edits to any button.

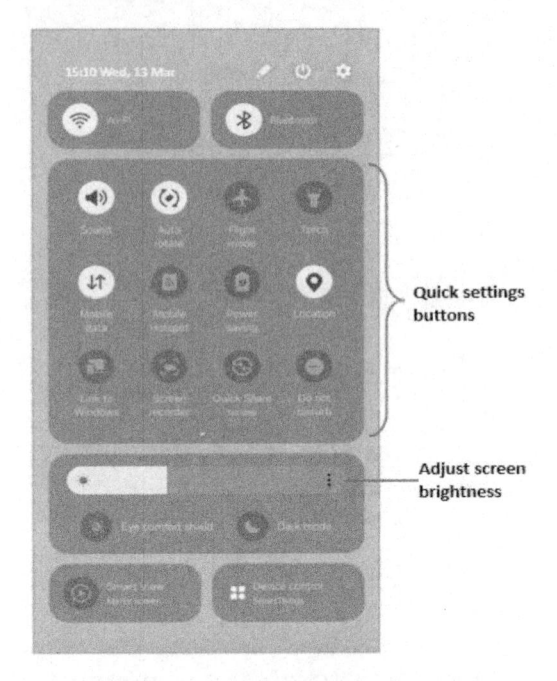

Controlling media playback

With the Media feature, you can take total control of your music or video playback. You can also continue playback on another device.

1. Open the notification panel and click **Media output**.
2. Tap the icons on the controller to take charge and control the playback.
3. To continue the playback on another device, touch ⓘ and pick the device you want.

Controlling nearby devices

Launch swiftly and be in control of nearby connected devices and frequently used SmartThings devices and scenes on the notification panel.

1   Open the notification panel on your phone and tap **Device control**.

Nearby connected devices and SmartThings devices and scenes will show up.

2   Select a nearby device or a SmartThings device to control it, or select a scene to launch it.

Entering text

Keyboard layout

A keyboard displays automatically when you enter text.

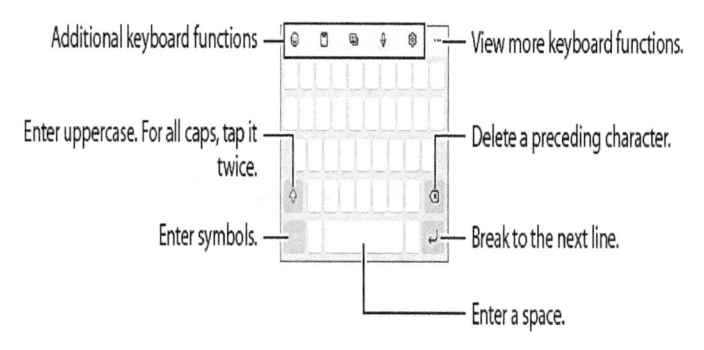

Additional keyboard functions — View more keyboard functions.

Enter uppercase. For all caps, tap it twice. — Delete a preceding character.

Enter symbols. — Break to the next line.

Enter a space.

NOTE: Not all languages support Text entry. To enter text, you must first of all change the input language to one that is supported.

Changing the input language

To change language, tap ⚙ the settings cog, then tap **Languages and types** > **Manage input languages** and pick the languages to use. When you select two or more languages, you can switch from one input language to another by swiping to the left or right on the space key.

Changing the keyboard

To change the keyboard, open the navigation bar and tap ⌨ the keyboard icon.

To change the keyboard type, tap the settings cog, ⚙ > **Languages and types**, pick a language, and then select the keyboard type you wish to use.

NOTE:

- If the keyboard button (⌨) does not show on the navigation bar, start the **Settings** app, click **General management** > **Keyboard list and default**, and then click **Keyboard button on navigation bar** switch to activate the feature.
- On a 3 x 4 keyboard, a key comprises of three or four characters. To input a character, click the corresponding key repeatedly until the desired character appears.

Copying and pasting

1. Tap and hold over the text you want to copy.
2. Drag 🔵 🔵 to the extent you wish to highlight the desired text, or tap **Select all** to select all text.
3. Click **Copy** or **Cut**.

   The text you have highlighted will be copied to the clipboard.
4. Touch and hold the area where the text is to be pasted and click **Paste** to insert the copied text.

   To paste text that has already been copied, just tap **Clipboard** and select the given text.

Additional keyboard functions

- ☺ : Enter stickers. You can also input your emoji stickers that look like you. Check out *Using your emoji stickers in chats* for more details.
- [GIF] : Attach animated GIFs.
- 🎤 : Enter text by voice.
- ⚙ : Change the keyboard settings.
- [A⇄] : Translate text and enter it in.
- 📋 : Add an item from the clipboard.
- ▯ : Switch to one-handed mode.

- ⌨: Change the keyboard mode.
- T: Recognize text from documents or images and insert it.
- +: Edit the keyboard function list.
- Tap the ellipsis ••• to use more keyboard functions.

CHAPTER 4
COMMUNICATIONS

The Phone app

The Phone app enables you to make/answer voice and video calls.

NOTE:

- If the part around the rear camera is covered, unwanted noises may be experienced during a call.
- Remove any accessories like screen protector and stickers close to the back camera.

Making calls

1. Open the **Phone** app and tap **Keypad**.
2. Enter a phone number.
3. Tap 🔵 to make a voice call, or tap 🎥 or 🎥 if you want to make a video call.

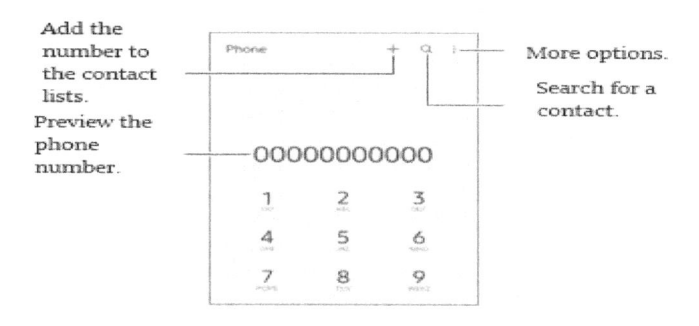

```
Add the
number to
the contact      Phone              +  Q  ⋮ ── More options.
lists.                                         Search for a
Preview the                                    contact.
phone            ──── 00000000000
number.
                      1    2    3
                      4    5    6
                      7    8    9
```

Making calls from call logs or contacts list

Open the **Phone** app, tap **Recents** or **Contacts**, and then swipe to the right on a contact or a phone number to make a call.

If this feature is not activated, tap ⋮ → **Settings** → **Other call settings**, followed by a tap on **Swipe to call or text** switch to activate it.

Using speed dial

To assign a number to speed dial, open the **Phone** app, tap **Keypad** or **Contacts**→⋮→**Speed dial numbers**, pick a speed dial number, after which you add a phone number.

To make a call, simply click and hold a speed dial number on the keypad. For speed dial numbers from 10 upwards, click the first digit(s) of the number, and then tap and hold the last digit.

For example, if you set the number 456 as a speed dial number, tap 4, tap 5, and then tap and hold 6.

Making an international call

1 Open the **Phone** app and click **Keypad**.
2 Touch and hold **0** until it changes to the plus (+) sign.
3 Type in the country code, area code, and phone number, and then tap 📞.

Receiving calls

How to answer a call

When you have an incoming call, drag 🕻 outside the large circle to receive the call.

How to reject a call

When you have an incoming call, drag ☎ outside the large circle to reject the call.

If you wish to send a message when rejecting an incoming call, drag the **Send message** bar upwards and choose a message to send.

To create different rejection messages, open the **Phone** app, tap ⋮ → **Settings** → **Quick decline messages**, type a message, and then tap ＋.

Blocking phone numbers

Block calls from precise numbers added to your block list.

1 Open the **Phone** app and tap ⋮ → **Settings** → **Block numbers**.

2 Tap **Recents** or **Contacts**, pick the contacts or phone numbers, and then tap **Done**. To manually enter a number, tap **Add phone number**, type in a phone number, and then tap ＋.

When blocked numbers attempt to reach you, you will not receive notifications. You will find the calls in the call log.

NOTE:

If you like to block incoming calls from people who hide their caller ID, just tap the **Block unknown/private numbers** switch to activate the feature.

Options during calls

- **Add call**: you can dial a second call while making a call. The first call will be placed on hold. When you end the second call, the first call will resume.

- **Hold call**: Place a call on hold.

- **Bluetooth**: Shift to a Bluetooth headset if it is connected to the device.

- **Speaker**: You may wish to activate or deactivate the speakerphone. When you are using the speakerphone, do not keep the device close to your ears.

- **Mute**: When you turn off the microphone, the other party will not be able to hear you.

- **Keypad/Hide**: Open or close keypad.

- Tap to end the current call.

- Tap to switch to a voice call from a video call

- **Camera**: During a video call, if you turn off the camera, the other party cannot see you.

- **Switch**: During a video call, you can switch between the front and back cameras.

- Select ⊙ to set your phone to automatically adjust the angle and zoom by identifying and tracking individuals during a video call.

- Tap 🔒 to lock the screen when making a video call.

- Select ✳ to change the screen ration while making a video call.

- **Effects**: Use this feature to apply different effects during a video call.

NOTE: Some features may be restricted depending on the service provider or model.

The Contacts app

This app enables you to create new contacts or manage contacts on the device.

Various ways to add contacts to your contact list on your Galaxy A55 5G

Create a new contact

1. Open the **Contacts** app and tap ✛.

2. Pick a storage location.

3. Input contact information and tap **Save**.

Import contacts from other sources

You may also like to add contacts by importing them from other storage media to your device.

1. Open the **Contacts** app and click the **Menu icon** ☰, select **Manage contacts**, then tap **Import contacts**.
2. Follow the instructions that display on the screen to import contacts.

Syncing contacts with your web accounts

You can set your device contacts to synchronize with online contacts saved in your web accounts, such as your Samsung account or Google account. Just follow the simple steps outlined below:

1. Open the **Settings** app, tap **Accounts and backup**, then tap **Manage accounts** and choose the account to sync with.
2. Tap **Sync account** and tap the **Contacts** switch to get it activated.

Searching for contacts

Open the **Contacts** app. Tap 🔍 at the top of the contacts menu and enter search criteria.

Tap the contact, and then take an action from the following options:

- ◯ : Make a voice call.
- ◯ / ◯ : Make a video call.
- ◯ : Compose a message.
- ◯ : Compose an email.

Deleting contacts

1   When you open the **Contacts** app, tap on the **More options** tab, ⋮ and select **Edit**.
2   Select the contacts you wish to delete and tap **Delete**.

To delete contacts one by one, tap a contact from the contacts menu and tap **More** → **Delete**.

Sharing contacts

You can your share contacts with others by using several sharing options:

1   When you open the **Contacts** app, tap on the **More options** tab, ⋮ and select **Edit**.
2   Choose contacts and tap **Share**.
3   Choose a method to share with.

Creating groups

If you like to add groups, such as family or friends, and manage contacts by group, follow these steps:

1. Open the **Contacts** app and tap the **Menu** tab ☰, then select **Groups,** and then **Create group.**
2. Follow the on-screen directives to create a group.

Merging duplicate contacts

If you have duplicated contacts in your list, merge them into one to update your contacts list.

1. Open the **Contacts** app and tap ☰ →**Manage contacts** → **Merge contacts.**
2. Tick contacts and tap **Merge.**

The Messages app

This is the app that lets you send and view messages by conversation.

You may need to pay additional charges for sending or receiving messages while roaming.

Sending messages

1. Open the **Messages** app and tap ⓐ.
2. Add recipients and enter a message.

If you like to record and send a voice message, tap and hold ᐧ�IIᐧ, say your message, and then release your finger from the icon. The recording icon will only appear when the message input field is empty.

3. Tap 🔘 to send the message.

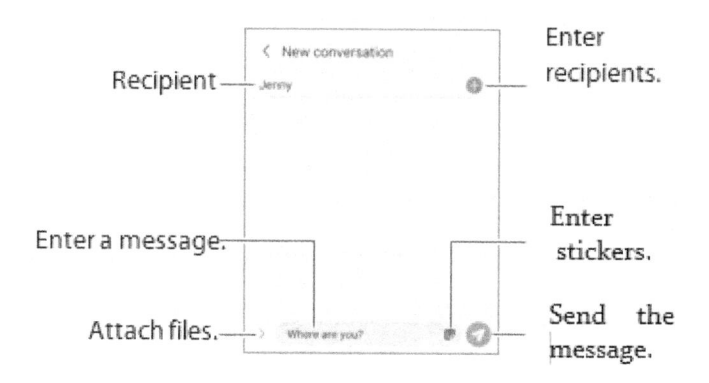

Recipient — Enter recipients.

Enter a message. — Enter stickers.

Attach files. — Send the message.

Viewing messages

1. Open the **Messages** app and tap **Conversations**.
2. On the message menu, pick a contact or a phone number.

- If you're replying to the message, tap the message input field, enter a message, and then tap send [🔘].
- To adjust the font size, drag two fingers apart or pinch on the screen.

79

Sorting messages

You can sort messages by category and manage them without stress.

Open the **Messages** app and tap **Conversations** and tap the plus sign (+) to add category.

If the category option does not show, tap ⋮ > **Settings** and tap the **Conversations categories** switch for it to be activated.

Deleting messages

Just tap and hold a message to delete, then tap **Delete**.

Changing message settings

Mount the **Messages** app, tap ⋮ > **Settings**. Here, you can also block unwanted messages, change notification settings, and so on.

Internet

Here, browsing the Internet to search for information and bookmarking your favorite web pages to access them is fun.

1 Launch the **Internet** app.
2 Type in the web address or a keyword, and then tap **Go**. For you to view the toolbars, just drag your finger downwards a little on the screen.

If you want to switch between tabs swiftly, swipe to the left or right on the address field.

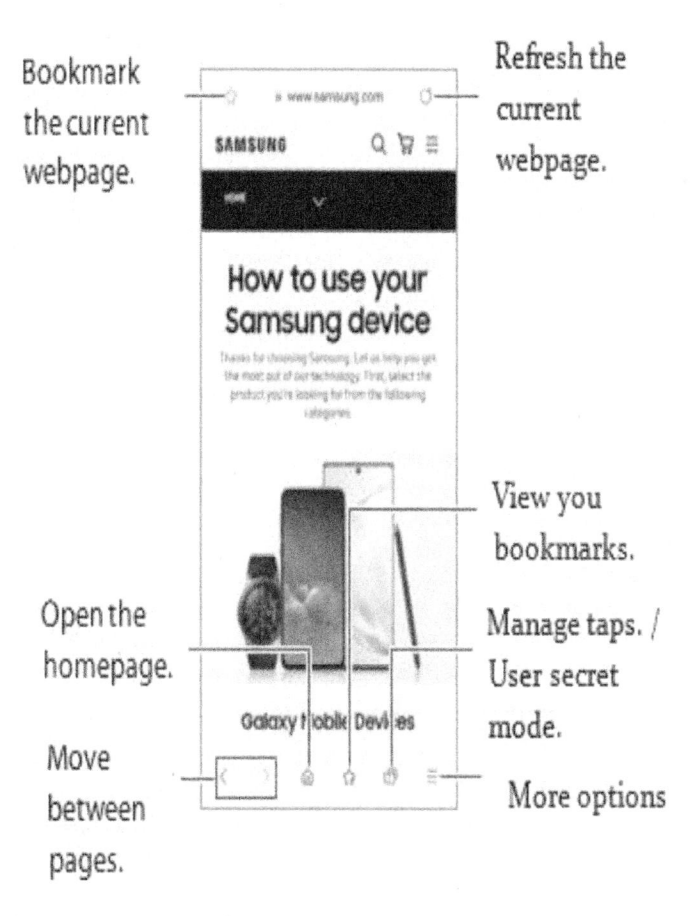

Bookmark the current webpage.

Refresh the current webpage.

View you bookmarks.

Open the homepage.

Manage taps. / User secret mode.

Move between pages.

More options

Using secret mode

You can prevent others from viewing your search history, browsing history, bookmarks, and saved pages by setting a password for secret mode.

1. Touch 🗇→**Turn on Secret mode**.
2. Touch the **Lock Secret mode** switch to activate it, touch **Start**, and then set a password for secret mode.

   In secret mode, the device will normally change the color of the toolbars. Anytime you want to deactivate secret mode, touch 🗇 → **Turn off Secret mode**.

NOTE: In secret mode, some features, such as screen capture may not be available.

CHAPTER 5
THE CAMERA AND GALLERY APPS

Camera

Capture pictures and record videos with various modes and settings.

Camera etiquette

- Do not take pictures or record videos of other people unless they have permitted you to do so.
- Do not take pictures or record videos in places where it is legally forbidden.
- Do not take pictures or record videos in places where your action may result in violation of other people's privacy.

How to take pictures with your Galaxy A55 5G

1. Open the **Camera** app.

    You can also launch the app by pressing the Side key twice quickly or by dragging the camera icon (◉) to the left on the locked screen.

2. Touch the image on the preview screen where you want the camera to focus.

- To adjust the brightness of pictures, pull the adjustment bar that displays above or below the circular frame.

3 Tap ◯ to take a picture.

- To alter the shooting mode, pull the shooting modes list to the left or right, or swipe either to the left or right on the preview screen.

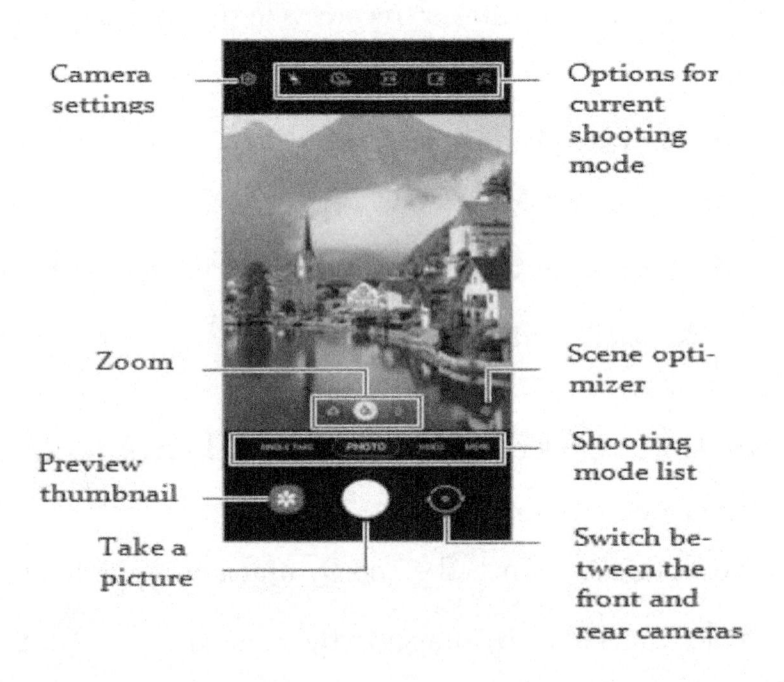

Camera settings — Options for current shooting mode

Zoom — Scene optimizer

Preview thumbnail — Shooting mode list

Take a picture — Switch between the front and rear cameras

NOTE:

- Some features of the camera are absent when you launch the **Camera** app from the locked screen or when the screen is turned off if your device has its screen lock method set.

- The camera automatically shuts off when it's not in use.
- Some methods may be absent depending on the service provider or model.
- The preview screen may differ based on the shooting mode and the type of camera being used.
- High resolution and high zoom ratio decrease the clarity of pictures and videos when taken from a close range. Therefore, maintain a good distance when taking pictures or videos.
- If you take pictures and they appear blurry, clean the camera lens and try taking again.
- Ensure that the lens is never damaged or contaminated. Or else, the device may not work well in some modes requiring high resolutions.
- Your device's camera possesses a wide-angle lens. Slight alteration may occur in wide-angle pictures or videos and does not imply device performance problems. To correct any alteration in pictures, tap the **Settings wheel** ⚙ on the preview screen, touch **Format and**

advanced options, and then touch the **Ultrawide shape correction** switch to make it activated.
- The highest capacity for video recording may differ depending on the resolution.
- If the device is exposed to sudden changes in air temperature, the camera may fog up or form condensation as a result of the difference in temperature outside and inside the camera cover. Take caution to avoid such conditions when planning to use the camera. If fogging occurs, allow the camera to dry naturally at room temperature before taking pictures or recording videos, otherwise results may look blurry.

How to use the zoom features on your Galaxy A55 5G

Select **.5x/1x/10x** or pull it to the left or right to zoom in or out respectively. Alternatively, drag your two fingers apart on the screen to zoom in, and tweak to zoom out.

NOTE:

- **.5x**: The Ultra-wide camera allows you to take wide-angle pictures or record wide-angle videos of things such as landscapes.
- **1x**: The wide-angle camera allows you to take basic pictures or record normal simple videos.
- **10x**: The telephoto camera enables you to take pictures or record videos by increasing the subject size.
- You can only make use of the zoom features when using the rear camera.

Locking the focus (AF) and exposure (AE)

You can lock the focus or exposure on a selected portion to inhibit the camera from automatically adjusting based on changes to the subjects or light sources.

Tap and hold the portion to focus, the AF/AE frame will display on the portion and the focus and exposure setting will be locked. The setting will still remain locked even after you take a picture.

NOTE: The availability of this feature is subject to the shooting mode.

How to use the camera button

- Touch and hold the camera button to record a video.

- If you like to take burst shots, simply swipe the camera button to the edge of the screen and hold it.

- Create GIFs by tapping the **Settings** icon ⚙ on the preview screen and selecting the option "**Swipe Shutter button to**", and then "**Create GIF**".

- If you've added another camera button, you can move it anywhere on the screen and take pictures more handily. On the preview screen, touch ⚙ → **Shooting methods** and touch the **Floating Shutter button** switch to activate it.

Options for current shooting mode

On the preview screen, make use of the following options:

- ⚡ : To activate or deactivate the flash.

- ⏱ : Choose how long to delay before the camera automatically takes a picture.

- 3:4 : Choose an aspect ratio and resolution for your pictures.

- 12M : Select a desired resolution for taking photos

- ▶ : To activate or deactivate the motion photo feature. If this feature is activated, a video clip will also be taken from a few seconds before tapping the camera button.

- ⁕ : To activate or deactivate the super steady feature to calm a video.
- AUTO : To pick a frame rate.
- ⌛∞ : Change the recording time for hyperlapse videos.
- 9:16 : Choose an aspect ratio for videos.
- FHD 30 : Choose a resolution for videos.
- ◈ : To apply any filter effect or beauty effects.
- ◎ : To choose a metering method. This controls how light values are calculated. ◎**Centre-weighted** makes use of the light in the center portion of the shot to determine the exposure of the shot. (o) **Spot metering** makes use of the light in a concentrated center portion of the shot to determine the exposure of the shot. (◊) **Matrix metering** takes the average the entire scene.

- ⬦ : In **FOOD** mode, instructing to focus on a subject within the circular frame and blur the image outside the frame.
- ⊕ : Instructing to regulate the color tone.
- 🌡 : Adjust the color temperature in **FOOD** mode
- ⊷ : To customize various shooting options during single take shots.
- ⬇ : To change the saving mode in **DUAL REC** mode.
- ⬚ : To change the screen in **DUAL REC** mode.

NOTE: The options available may differ according to the model or shooting mode.

How to use the Photo mode on Galaxy A55 5G

The camera regulates the shooting options automatically based on the immediate surroundings to capture pictures easily.

From the shooting modes menu, tap **PHOTO** and tap ○ to take a picture.

Taking high-resolution pictures

Take high-resolution pictures following these simple steps:

In the shooting options, tap **12M**, then choose the resolution you want to use and take a picture.

NOTE: If this feature has not been activated, tap ⚙ on the preview screen and tap the **Scene optimizer** switch to activate it.

Shot suggestions

The camera recommends the ideal composition for the picture by identifying the position and angle of your subject.

On the preview screen, click ⚙ and touch the **Shot suggestions** switch to activate it.

1. On the shooting modes list, click **PHOTO**.

    A guide will display on the preview screen.

2. Point the guide directly at the subject.

    The camera will recognize the composition, and the recommended composition will display on the preview screen.

3. Move the device around until the guide matches the recommended composition.

    When the ideal composition is attained, the guide will change its color to yellow.

4. Tap ○ to take a picture.

How to take selfies with your new Galaxy A55 5G phone

You can take self-portraits with the front camera of your smartphone.

1. On the preview screen, swipe upwards or downwards, or click ⊙ to switch to the front camera for self-portraits.

2. Face the front camera lens.

If you want to take self-portraits with a wide-angle shot of the landscape or people, click 😊.

3. Click ◯ to take a picture.

How to Apply filter and beauty effects to your shots

You can choose a filter effect and alter facial features, such as your skin tone or face shape, before actually taking a picture.

1. On the preview screen, click ◈.
2. Choose effects and take a picture.

You can tap ⊕ to download filters from the **Galaxy Store**, or if you like, you can use the **My filters style** to create your own filter by using an image with a color tone you love from the **Gallery app**.

Video mode

The camera will adjust the shooting options automatically in relation on the surroundings to record videos easily.

1. On the shooting modes menu, click **VIDEO** and click ⦿ to record a video.

   - To switch from the front to the rear camera and vice versa while recording, swipe upwards or downwards on the preview screen or click ⟳

   - To snap an image from the video while recording, click the Capture button ◯.

2. Tap the **Stop button** ■ to stop recording the video.

Please note that the optical zoom feature may not function well in a low-light environment.

Stabilizing videos (Super steady)

This feature enables you to stabilize videos when recording.

To use the feature, simply tap **VIDEO** on the shooting modes menu, activate it by tap 🏃 on the shooting options, and afterwards, record a video.

How to use the auto framing feature on your Galaxy A55 5G

With the auto framing function, which allows you to adjust the shooting angle and zoom by monitoring individuals, you are able to program the device to automatically change the shooting angle and zoom by tracking people while recording a video.

To begin recording a video, select **VIDEO** from the list of shooting modes and then toggle it on by tapping ⊙.

How to record with Dual rec mode

Use two cameras simultaneously to record videos. Each camera's video can be edited and saved independently. Additionally, you have the option of playing the videos in split view or picture-in-picture mode.

1. From the shooting modes list, select **MORE** > **DUAL REC**.
   - If you don't want to save the videos as one, click ⬇ to choose the option to save the videos of each camera separately.

- Click ⬚ at the top left corner to switch between the main **Preview** screen and the **Picture-in-picture view** screen.

3. Click ⦿ to start recording a video
4. Click ■ to stop video recording.

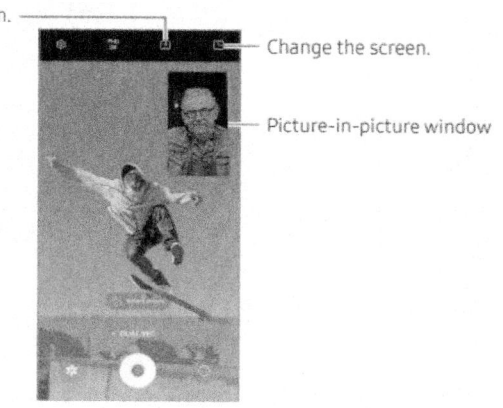

Change the saving option.

Change the screen.

Picture-in-picture window

Portrait mode

The camera enables you to take shots where the background is blurred and the subject stands out clearly.

1 Tap **PORTRAIT** from the shooting modes menu.

2 Tap ⦿ and move the background blur adjustment bar to adjust the blur level.

3 As soon as you see **Ready** appear on the preview screen, tap the capture button ◯ to take a picture.

Background blur adjustment bar

NOTE:

- This feature is best used in a place with sufficient light.
- The background blur may be poorly applied due to the following conditions:

— The device or the subject is moving.

— The subject is thin or transparent.

— The subject has a similar color to the background.

— The subject or background is plain.

Fun mode

Take a picture with numerous effects.

1. On the shooting modes list, click **FUN**.
2. To choose a different effect, slide the camera button to the left or right.

3. Tap on the effect button to take a photo or touch and hold the effect button to record a video.

Pro mode / Pro video mode

Capture pictures or videos as you manually adjust different shooting options, such as exposure value and ISO value.

From the shooting modes menu, click **MORE→PRO** or **PRO VIDEO**. Choose options and customize the settings, and then click ○ to take a picture or click ◉ to record a video.

Available options

○ : Reset the settings.

ISO : Choose an ISO value. This regulates camera light sensitivity. Smaller ISO values are used for stationary or well luminous objects. Higher values are used for fast-moving objects or objects with poor illumination. Nevertheless, higher ISO settings can cause noise in pictures or videos.

SPEED: Regulate the shutter speed. A slow shutter speed lets more light in, so the picture or video becomes brighter. This is perfect for pictures or videos of scenery or pictures or videos taken at night. A fast shutter speed lets less light in. This is perfect for capturing pictures or videos of fast-moving subjects.

EV : Change the exposure value. This controls how much light the camera's sensor receives. For low-light occasions, use a higher exposure.

FOCUS: Change the focus mode. Move the adjustment bar towards or to adjust the focus by yourself to satisfaction.

WB : Select a suitable white balance, to make your images have a true-to-life color range. You can also set the color temperature.

Separating the focus area and the exposure area

It is possible to separate the focus area and the exposure area.

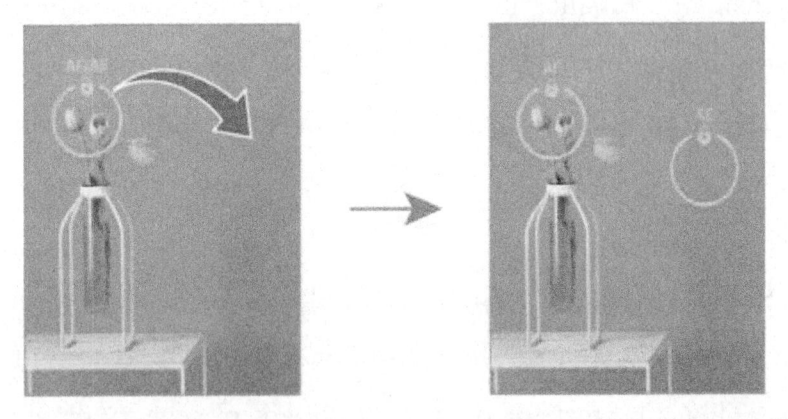

Click and hold the preview screen. The AF/AE frame will display on the screen. Move the frame to the place where you want to separate the focus area and the exposure area.

Single take mode

The Single take mode lets you take different pictures and videos in just a single shot.

Your device automatically selects the best shot and generates pictures with filters or videos with certain segments repeated.

1 From the shooting modes list, click **MORE**, then **SINGLE TAKE**.

2 Click ○ and move the camera to capture the scene you like to capture.

3 When you're done, click the preview thumbnail.

To look at other results, tap on ⌒ icon. If you like to save the results separately, touch and hold an item, mark the items you want, and then tap ↓.

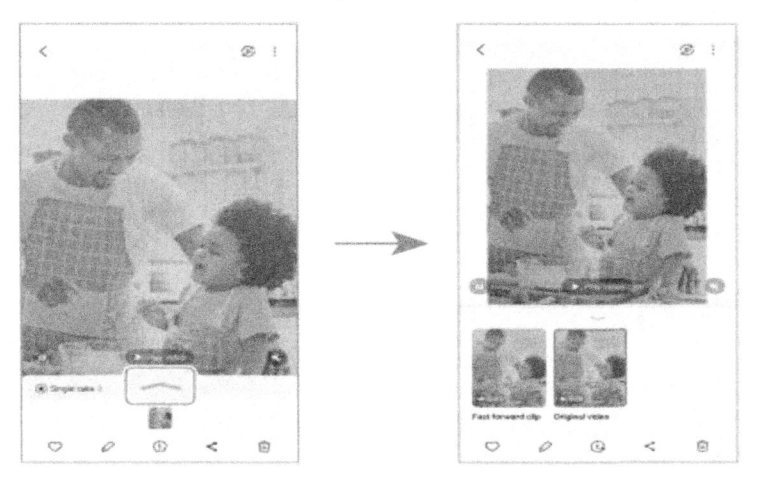

Night mode

Take a picture in low-light environment, without using the flash. When you use a tripod, you can get better results.

1   From the shooting modes menu, tap **MORE→NIGHT**.

2   Click ◯ and hold your device stable until shooting is complete.

Food mode

You can capture pictures of food with more lively colors.

1. From the shooting modes menu, click **MORE→FOOD**.

2. Touch the screen and pull the circular frame over the area to highlight.

   The area outside the circular frame will be hazy.

   To resize the circular frame, move a corner of the frame.

3. Tap 🌡 and move the adjustment bar to adjust the color tone.

4. Click ◯ to take a picture.

Panorama mode

You can take a series of pictures and then stitch them together to create a wide scene using the panorama mode.

1. From the shooting modes menu, click **MORE** → **PANORAMA**.

2. Click ◯ and move the device slowly in one direction. Retain the image inside the frame on the camera's viewfinder. If the preview image is not inside the guide frame or you don't move the device, the device will automatically cease to take pictures.

3. Click ◯ to stop taking pictures.

NOTE: It's not advisable taking pictures of indistinct backgrounds, like an empty sky or a plain wall.

Macro mode

Allows you to pictures of subjects at close range.

From the shooting modes menu, click **MORE** → **MACRO**.

Super Slow-mo mode

Super slow motion is a feature that enables you to record a fast passing moment slowly so that you can appreciate it later.

1 From the shooting modes menu, click **MORE** → **SUPER SLOW-MO** and click ⬤ to record a video. The device will record the instance in super slow motion and save it as a video.

2   From the preview screen, click the preview thumbnail and click **Play super slow-mo video**. If you want to edit the super slow motion section, tap the pencil icon ⌀ and shift the section editing bar to the left or right.

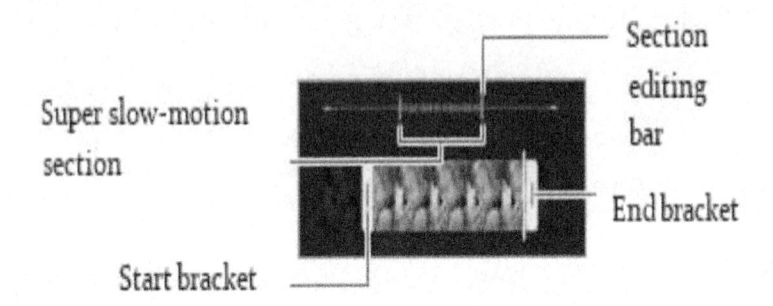

Super slow-motion section

Section editing bar

End bracket

Start bracket

NOTE: Use this feature in an environment that has enough light. When recording a video indoors with inadequate or poor lighting, the screen may appear dark or be gritty. The screen may glimmer in certain lighting situations, such as in areas with fluorescent lighting.

Slow motion mode

Record a video to view it in slow motion. You can stipulate segments of your videos to be played in slow motion.

1. From the shooting modes menu, tap **MORE→SLOW MOTION** and tap ⦿ to record a video.

2. When you are done recording, tap ⦿ to stop.

102

3. On the preview screen, click the preview thumbnail and click **Play slow motion video**.

The fast segment of the video will be set as a slow-motion segment and the video will start playing. Up to two slow motion segments will be created according to the video.

To edit the slow-motion segment, tap the pencil icon ✏ and move the segment editing bar to the left or right.

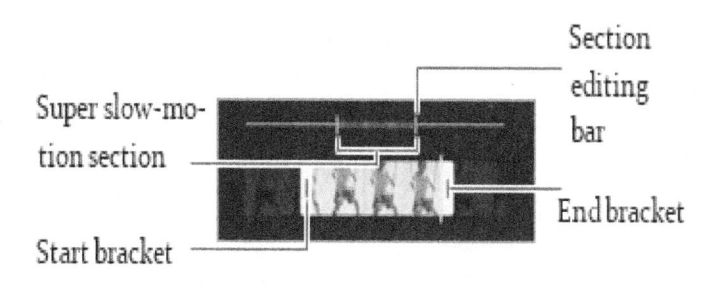

Super slow-motion section

Start bracket

Section editing bar

End bracket

Hyperlapse mode

This feature enables you to record scenes, like passing people or cars, and view them as fast-motion videos.

1. On the shooting modes menu, click **MORE** → **HYPERLAPSE**.
2. Tap **AUTO** and pick a frame rate option.

If you set the frame rate to **AUTO**, the device will automatically regulate the frame rate depending on the changing rate of the scene.

Also, if you wish to record star trails, you can set the frame to **+300×** and then select ⊙.

3. Tap the start button ⊙ to begin the recording.
4. Tap the stop button ■ to complete recording.

Customizing camera settings

On the preview screen, click the settings cog ⚙. Some options may be unavailable based on the shooting mode you're currently on.

Intelligent features

- **Scene optimizer**: Helps to adjust the colour settings and apply the optimized effect automatically according to the subject or scene.
- **Shot suggestions**: Helps to suggest the perfect composition for the picture by identifying the position and angle of your subject.
- **Scan QR codes**: Enables the device to scan QR codes from the preview screen.

Pictures

- **Swipe Shutter button to**: Choose what happens when you swipe the camera button to the edge of the screen and hold it.
- **HEIF pictures**: Capture images in the High Efficiency Image Format (HEIF).
- **Watermark**: Add a watermark at the lower left corner of the screen when capturing images.

Selfies

- **Save selfies as previewed**: Configure the device to save images as they appear on the preview screen when captured with the front camera without flipping them.

Videos

- **High efficiency videos**: Record your videos in the High Efficiency Video Codec (HEVC) format. Your HEVC videos will be saved as compressed files to help you manage the device's memory.

NOTE:

- You will not be able to play the HEVC videos on other devices or share them online.
- You will not be able to record Super slow motion and slow motion videos in the HEVC format.

- **Video stabilization**: Activate anti-shake to minimize or eliminate blurry image ensuing from camera shake while recording a video.
- **Auto FPS**: This feature allows you to optimize the frame rate in such a way that the device automatically records brighter films even when the lighting is poor.

General
- **Auto HDR**: Capture images with rich colors and replicate details even in bright and dark areas.
- **Grid lines**: Show viewfinder guides to help composition when selecting subjects.
- **Location tags**: Attach a GPS location tag to the image.

NOTE:
- GPS signal strength may reduce in places where the signal is obstructed, such as between buildings or in low-lying areas, or in poor weather conditions.
- Your location may show on your pictures when you upload them to the Internet. To prevent this, deactivate the location tag setting.
- **Shooting methods**: Select several more shooting methods for capturing an image or recording a video.

- **Settings to keep**: Preserve the last settings you used, such as the shooting mode, when you mount the camera.
- **Storage location**: Choose the memory location for storage. This feature will display when you insert a memory card.
- **Vibration feedback:** Configure the smartphone to vibrate in specified conditions, such as when you press the camera button.
- **Show Snapchat Licenses in Fun mode**: Automate the device to capture a photo with different effects with special unique Snapchat Lenses.

Privacy
- **Privacy Notice**: View the privacy notice.
- **Permissions**: View the permissions needed to operate the Camera app.
- **Reset settings**: Reset the camera settings
- **About Camera**: Check the Camera app version and legal information.
- **Contact us**: Ask questions or see frequently asked questions

Screenshotting and screen recording on the Galaxy A55 5G

Feel like capturing a screenshot while using the device and lovingly write on, draw on, crop, or share the captured screen? Simple!

How to capture a screenshot on your new Galaxy A55 5G

Use the following simple approaches to capture a screenshot. You'll be able to view the captured screenshots in **Gallery**.

Approach 1) Button capture: Press the Side button and the Volume Down button simultaneously.

Approach 2) Swipe capture: Swipe the edge of your hand to the left or right just across the device's screen.

NOTE:

- You'll not be able to capture a screenshot while using some apps and features.

- If capturing a screenshot by swiping is not yet activated in your device, launch the **Settings** app, tap **Advanced features** > **Motions and gestures**, and then tap the **Palm swipe to capture** switch to activate it.

After taking a screenshot, select from the following options on the toolbar at the bottom of the screen:

- ⌊⌄⌋ : Allows you to capture the current content and the hidden content on an extended page, such as a webpage. When you tap ⌊⌄⌋, the screen automatically scrolls down to capture more contents.

- ✏️ : Enables you to write or draw on the screenshot or crop a section from the screenshot. You can then view the cropped area in **Gallery**.

- # : This will help you add some tags to the screenshot. To find screenshots by tag, tap the **Search** icon Q in the **Gallery app**. There you'll see the tags list and quickly find any screenshot you're looking for.

- ◁ : Lets you share the screenshot with others.

NOTE: If you do not see the options on the captured screen, simply go to the **Settings** app, tap **Advanced features > Screenshots and screen recorder**, and then tap the **Screenshot toolbar** switch to activate it. And there you are!

Screen record

Would you like to record the screen while using your device? Follow the simple steps:

1. Open the notification panel,
2. Swipe downwards,
3. Tap ⊙ (**Screen recorder**) to activate it.
4. Choose a sound setting and tap **Start recording**. You'll have a countdown, after which recording will start.

   - If you want to write or draw on the screen, simply tap ✎.
   - If you to record a video of yourself, tap 👤

5. After recording the video, tap ■ to stop.

Your video will be automatically saved in **Gallery**.

NOTE: To modify the screen recorder settings, launch the **Settings** app and tap **Advanced features** > **Screenshots and screen recordings**.

How to extract text from images

When working with some apps like the camera app or the Gallery app, you may find the need to extract some text from images and copy it elsewhere or share it in other apps. To do this, follow these steps:

Step 1: On an image where there is text to be extracted, e.g. in **Gallery**, you'll see the text icon ● as shown in the illustration below. Tap the icon.

Step 2: Go ahead and select the area to extract the text.

Step 3: Choose an option to copy, select all or share.

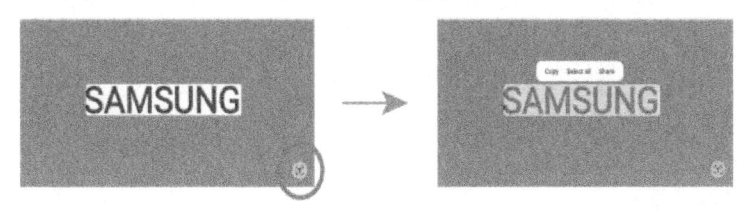

Gallery

Here, you can explore images and videos stored in your device. You can also manage images and videos according to album or create stories.

Using Gallery

Launch the **Gallery** app to browse your images.

— More options

— Search for images and videos.

— Sync images and videos.

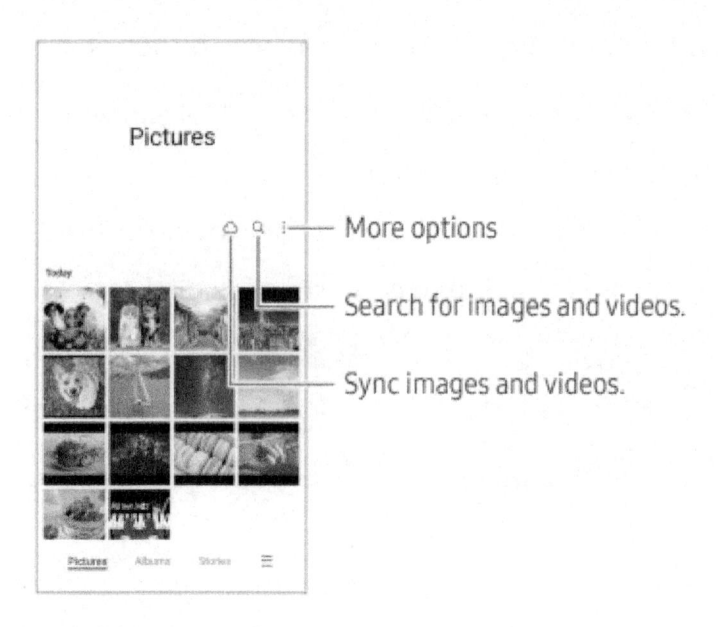

Grouping similar images

Open the **Gallery** app and click ▢ to group similar images and show only the best shots as a preview of the images. When you click the image preview, you'll be able to see all the images in the group.

Viewing images

Launch the **Gallery** app and choose an image. To see other files, swipe to the left or right on the screen.

Image and video thumbnail

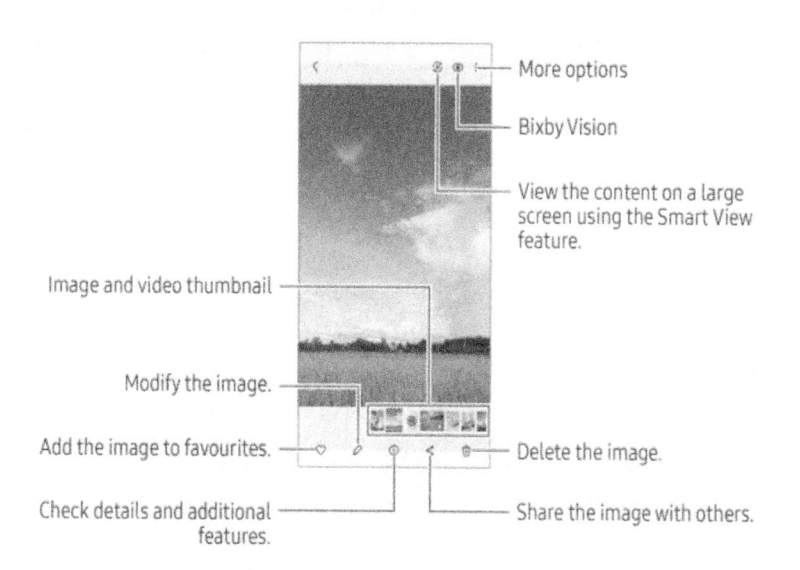

Modify the image.
Add the image to favourites.
Check details and additional features.

More options
Bixby Vision
View the content on a large screen using the Smart View feature.

Delete the image.
Share the image with others.

Remastering images

With the Galaxy A55 5G Camera, you can improve those dull, blurry, and low-resolution images with the remaster feature. With this feature, you can literally bring life into those dead photos. You can compare the remastered photo with the original one to see the difference for yourself.

To remaster an image, follow these simple steps:

1. Open the **Gallery** app and select the image you want to work on.

2. Tap the **Info** button ⓘ and select **Remaster**.

3. Tap the **Save** button ↓ to save your new image.

How to crop enlarged images in Gallery

1. Open the **Gallery** app and choose the image you want to crop.

2. Drag two fingers apart on the area you want to save and click ⊙.

The cropped area will automatically be saved for you as a file.

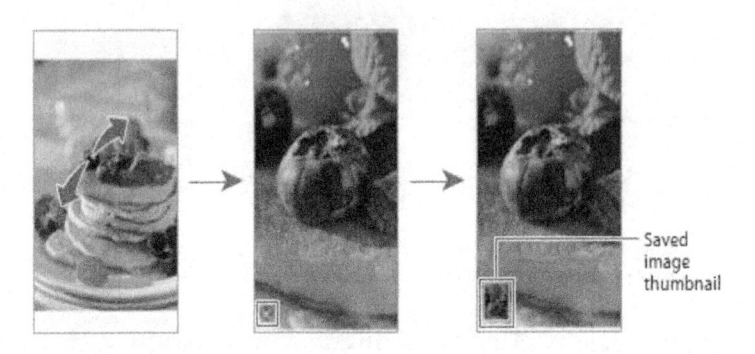

Saved image thumbnail

Viewing videos

Open the **Gallery** app and select a video to play. To view your other files, swipe to the left or right on the screen. To make use of several other options during playback, tap ⋮, then tap **Open in Video player**.

View the content on a large screen using the Smart View feature.

Skip to the previous video. Touch and hold to rewind.

Rewind or fast-forward by dragging the bar.

Capture the current screen.

Create a GIF.

Change the screen ratio.

Configure the caption settings.

More options

Skip to the next video. Touch and hold to fast-forward.

Pause and resume playback.

Lock the playback screen.

Rotate the screen.

Change the playback speed.

Switch to the pop-up video player.

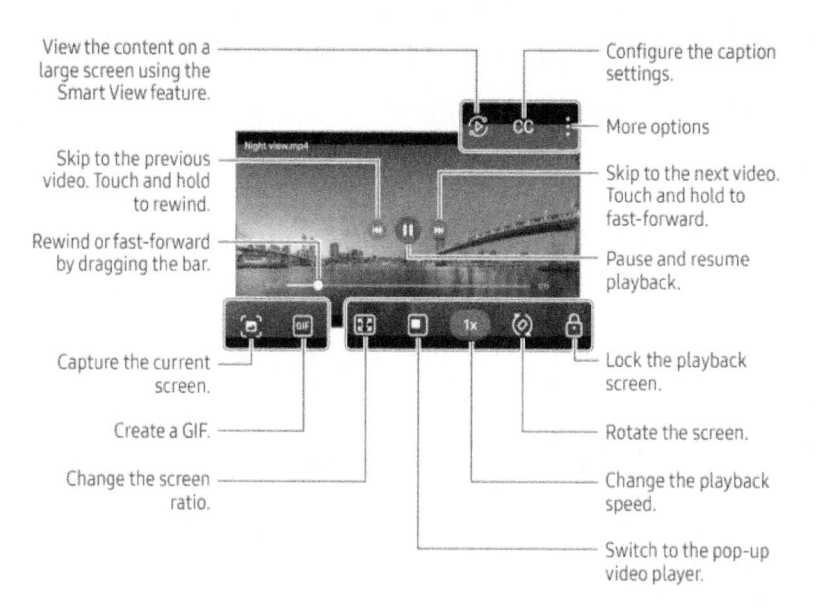

You can control the brightness of the playback by moving your finger up and down on the left side of the playback screen, and you can control the volume by moving your finger up and down on the right side of the playback screen. Swipe to the left or right side of the playback screen to rewind or fast-forward the recording, respectively.

Albums

Create albums and sort your images and videos.

1. To create an album, open the **Gallery** app, select **Albums**, select the **Add** button ✛, and then select **Album**.

2 Select the items (images or videos) you wish to copy or move the images to an album.

Stories

As you take pictures or record videos and store them to the device, it will read the date and location tags on them, organize the pictures and videos, and then make stories out of them.

Launch the **Gallery** app, navigate to the **Stories** tab, and then choose a story to see. If you tap on the **More options** tab ⋮, you'll have access to a variety of choices, such as altering the content of the story or changing the title of the story.

You are able to create stories manually by tapping the stories list menu ⋮. and selecting **Create story** option.

How to Sync images and videos on your device with your cloud account

Open the **Gallery** app, click the **cloud** icon ☁, and then follow the on-screen instructions to finish the sync. The **Gallery** app will be synced with the cloud.

When your **Gallery** app is synced with the cloud, your pictures and videos will also be saved in the cloud. You can view images and videos saved in the cloud in your **Gallery** app and from other devices any time.

NOTE: When you have your Samsung account and Microsoft account connected, you can set the cloud storage as Microsoft OneDrive.

Deleting images or videos

Open the **Gallery** app, touch and hold an image, a video, or a story you want to delete, and then click **Delete**.

Using the recycle bin feature

Reserve the deleted images and videos in the recycle bin. The files will be deleted after a given period.

Open the **Gallery** app, click the **Menu** icon ≡, select **Settings**, and then click the **Recycle bin** switch to activate it.

To view files in the recycle bin, open the **Gallery** app and click ≡, and then **Recycle bin**.

AR Zone

Introduction

AR Zone offers you AR related features. Choose a feature and capture exciting pictures or videos.

Learn how to launch and use the AR Zone

Use the following procedures to launch AR Zone:

- Open the **AR Zone** app.

- Open your phone's **Camera** app and tap **MORE**, then select **AR ZONE**.

Learn about AR Emoji Studio

How to create AR Emoji

Create an emoji that looks like you thus:

1. Open the **AR Zone** app and click **AR Emoji Studio**.
2. Position your face straight on the screen, tap ⭘ to take a selfie or swipe to the left or right to see various pre-made emojis, select one and then tap ⤳.
3. Follow the on-screen commands to create an emoji.

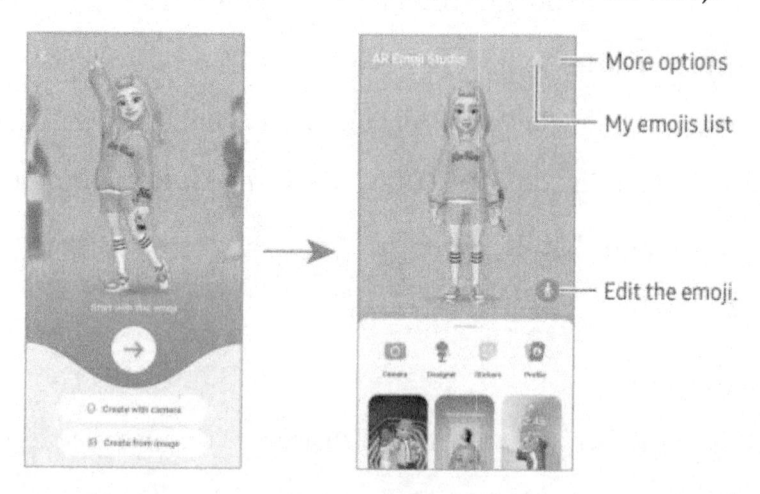

You can select the AR emoji you want to use in the **AR Zone** app by selecting **AR Emoji Studio** > 😃 , and then selecting an emoji of your choice.

Deleting an emoji

Open the **AR Zone** app and click **AR Emoji Studio,** then click ⃤ and then the bin icon 🗑. Tick the emoji you want to delete, and finally, click **Delete**.

Making an AR emoji short video and using it to decorate your device

You may utilize an emoji as a wallpaper or call background picture by making a short movie with it.

1. To access AR Emoji Studio, open the **AR Zone** app and select **AR Emoji Studio**.

2. Choose from three options: **Create video, Call screen,** or **Lock screen**.

3. Choose a template that you wish to use.

To change the background image, press ⬤ → 🖼.

4. To save the video, tap **Save**.

In the **Gallery**, you may see the videos you've saved.

5 Choose an option at the bottom of the screen to utilize the video immediately.

Using an AR emoji to create your contact profile

Use an emoji as your Samsung account's profile image and in the **Contacts** app. You may select from a variety of postures or make your own.

1. Open the **AR Zone** app and select **AR Emoji Studio** from the menu.
2. Go to **Profile** and choose an emoji.
3. Tap ○ to record your emotion or to choose a position.
4. Tap the **Done** button, and then **Save**.

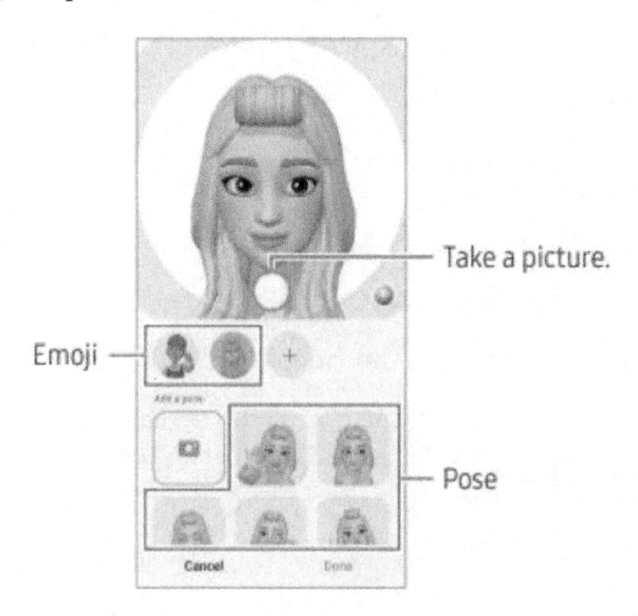

How to use the AR Emoji Camera to capture pictures or videos

Using a variety of camera modes, you may take interesting images or record entertaining videos with emojis.

1. Open the **AR Zone** app and click **AR Emoji Camera**.
2. Choose the emoji and the mode you want to use. The available modes may differ according to the emoji you choose.

    - **SCENE**: The emoji will mimic your expressions.
    - **MASK**: The emoji's face will appear over your face, making it look like you're wearing a mask.
    - **MIRROR**: The emoji will mimic your body movements.
    - **PLAY**: The emoji will move on a real background.

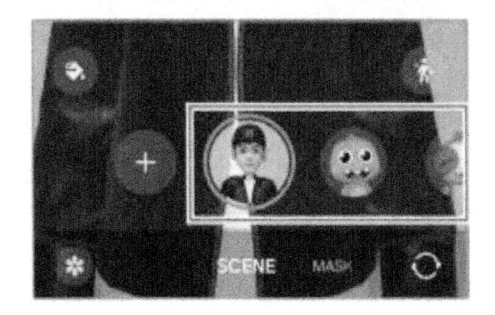

3. Click the emoji icon to capture a picture, or click and hold the icon to record a video.

You can view and share the pictures and videos that you have captured in your phone's **Gallery**.

Working with AR Emoji Stickers

Make your own stickers with your emoji's expressions and actions. You will be able to use your emoji stickers when sending messages or use them on a social network.

Creating your own stickers

1. Open the **AR Zone** app and click **AR Emoji Stickers**.
2. Click ＋ at the top of the stickers menu.
3. Edit stickers as you like and click **Save**.

   You can view the stickers you have made at the top of the stickers menu.

Deleting emoji stickers

Open the **AR Zone** app and click **AR Emoji Stickers**→⋮ →**Edit**. Choose the emoji stickers to delete and click **Delete**.

How to use your emoji stickers in chats

You can use your emoji stickers when having a conversation through messages or on a social network. The underlisted actions are an example of using your emoji stickers in the **Messages** app.

1 During a message composition in the **Messages** app, click ☺ on the Samsung keyboard.
2 Tick the emoji icon.
3 Choose any of your emoji stickers.

The emoji sticker will be inserted into the message.

Emoji icon

AR Doodle

Record fun videos with virtual handwriting or drawings on faces or any other part. As soon as the camera recognizes a face or space, the doodles on the face will then follow the face as it moves, and the doodles in the space will be fixed in the same place notwithstanding whether the camera moves.

1 Open the **AR Zone** app and tap **AR Doodle**.

When the camera recognizes the subject, the recognition area will display on the screen.

2. Write or draw in the recognition area by tapping ⬤.

- If you switch to the back camera, you can also write or draw outside the recognition area.

- If you tap ⬤ and then start doodling, you can record yourself doodling.

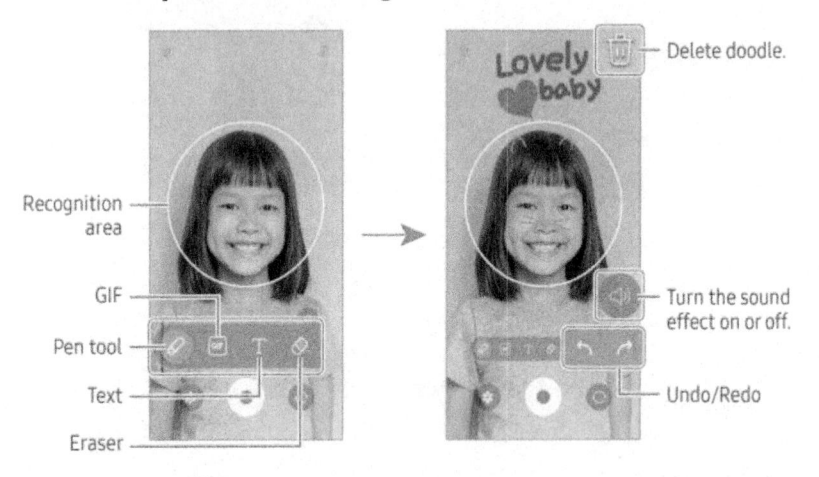

Recognition area
GIF
Pen tool
Text
Eraser

Delete doodle.
Turn the sound effect on or off.
Undo/Redo

3. Tap ⬤ to record a video.

4. Tap ⬛ to stop recording the video.

You can view and share the video in your **Gallery**.

NOTE: The particular features displayed on the preview screen depend on the camera that's in use.

CHAPTER 6
APPS AND FEATURES

Samsung Health

Samsung Health enables you manage your wellness and fitness. Define fitness goals, monitor your progress, and keep track of your overall wellness and fitness. You can also compare your step count records with other Samsung Health users and see other health tips. Please visit www.samsung.com/samsung-health for more details.

Using Samsung Health

Open the **Samsung Health** app. When you want to run this app for the first time or restart it after performing a data reset, use the on-screen guidelines to complete the setup.

To edit items on the Samsung Health home screen, click **Manage items** at the bottom of the trackers list.

Monitor your health and fitness.

Compare your step count records with other Samsung Health users or compete with your friends.

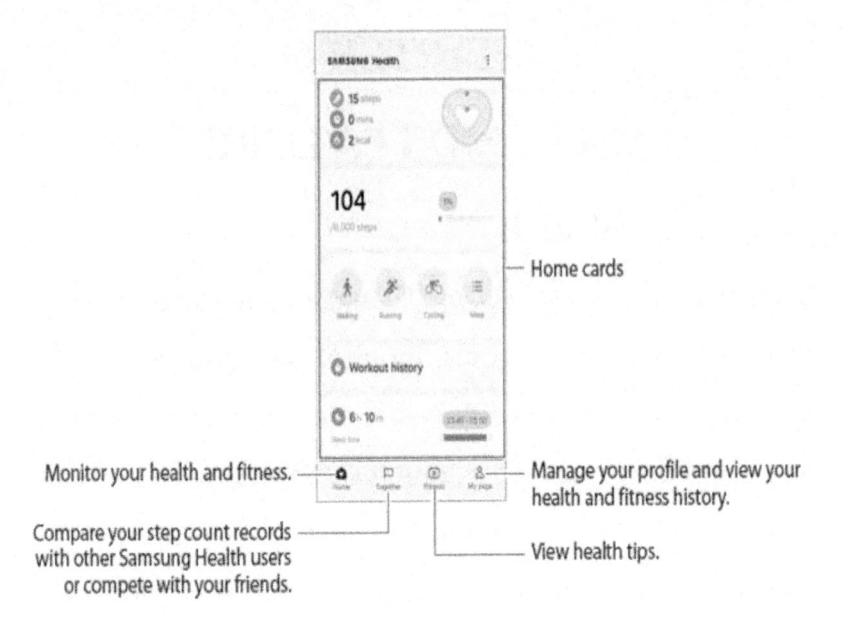

Manage your profile and view your health and fitness history.

View health tips.

Home cards

NOTE:

- Some features may be absent depending on the region.
- If you're using the steps tracker while travelling by car or train, your step count may affect your vibration.

Samsung Notes

Make notes by typing text from the keyboard or by handwriting or drawing on the screen. You can also insert your best-loved images or voice recordings into your notes.

Creating notes

1 Open the **Samsung Notes** app, click ⌨, and then create a note.

You can change the input method by clicking ⓐ or ⌨.

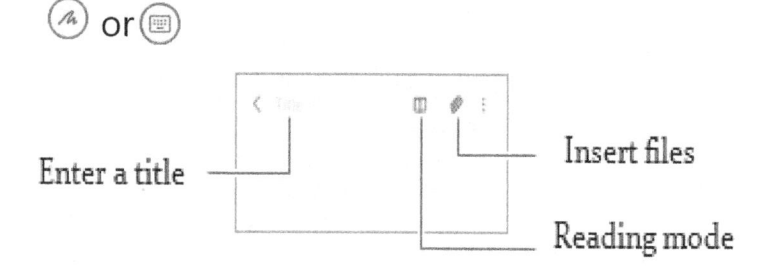

Enter a title ——— [diagram] ——— Insert files
                                  Reading mode

2 After composing the note, click the Back button to save it. If you want to save the note in another file format, touch ⋮→**Save as file**.

Deleting notes

Touch and hold a note to delete and click **Delete**.

Samsung Kids

You can restrict children's access to some particular apps, set their usage times, and configure settings to give an exciting and safe environment for children when they use the device.

Open the notification panel, swipe downwards, and then click ◉ (**Kids**) to activate the feature. The Samsung Kids screen will display. If it's not there, click the Edits menu button ✎, select **Edit,** and drag it over to add it. When you're using this feature for the first time or after performing a data reset, follow the on-screen instructions to complete the setup.

On the Samsung Kids screen, choose the app you want to use.

NOTE: Your preset screen lock method or your created PIN will be required when activating the **Parental controls** feature or closing Samsung Kids.

How to use the parental control features

You can configure the settings for Samsung Kids and check the usage history.

On the Samsung Kids screen, click ⋮→**Parental controls** and input your unlock code.

Closing Samsung Kids

To close Samsung Kids, click the Back button or click ⋮ →**Close Samsung Kids**, and then input your unlock code.

Galaxy Wearable

Galaxy Wearable is an app that lets you manage your wearable devices. When you connect your device to the wearable device, you can personalize the wearable device's settings and apps.

Open the **Galaxy Wearable** app.

Click the **More** > **Continue** to connect your device to the wearable device. Follow the on-screen instructions to finish the setup. Refer to the user manual of the specific wearable device for more information about how to connect and use it with your device.

Calendar

Manage your schedule by putting upcoming events in your planner.

Creating events

1. Open the **Calendar** app and click ⊕ or double-click a date.

   If the date already has saved events or tasks in it, click the date and click ⊕.

2. Enter event details and click **Save**.

Syncing events with your accounts

1. Open the **Settings** app, click **Accounts and backup** → **Manage accounts**, and then choose the account to sync with.

2. Click **Sync account** and click the **Calendar** switch to activate it.

To add accounts to sync with, open the **Calendar** app and click ≡→ ⚙→**Manage calendars**. Then click thee plus button ✚ to add account. Then, choose an account to sync with and sign in. When you add an account, a blue circle is displayed next to the account name.

Reminder

Register to-do items as reminders and get notifications according to the condition you set.

NOTE:
- To receive more exact notifications, connect to a Wi-Fi or mobile network.
- To use location reminders, you must activate the GPS feature. Location reminders may be unavailable depending on the model.

Starting Reminder

Open the **Calendar** app and click ☰ → **Reminder** → 🔔. The Reminder screen will display and the Reminder app icon (🔔) will be added to the Apps screen.

Creating reminders

1. Open the **Reminder** app.
2. Click **Write a reminder** or ⊕, input the details, and then click **Save**.

Completing reminders

On the reminders menu, click ⭕ or just choose a reminder and click **Complete**.

Restoring reminders

Restore reminders that have been completed.

1. On the reminders menu, click ≡ → **Completed**.
2. Choose a category and click **Edit**.
3. Mark items to restore and click **Restore**.

   Reminders will be included in the reminders list and you will be reminded again.

Deleting reminders

To delete a reminder, choose a reminder and click **Delete**.

To delete multiple reminders, click and hold a reminder, Mark reminders to delete, and then click **Delete**.

Voice Recorder

Record or play voice recordings.

1 Launch the **Voice Recorder** app.

2 Click ⏺ to start recording. Speak into the microphone.

- Click ⏸ to pause recording.

  - While making a voice recording, click **BOOKMARK** to insert a bookmark.

3 Click ⏹ to finish recording.

4   Type a file name and click **Save**.

Changing the recording mode on the Galaxy A55 5G

Choose a mode from the top of the voice recorder screen.

- **Standard**: This is the normal recording mode.
- **Speech-to-text**: The device records your voice and instantly converts it to on-screen text. For best results, place the device close to your mouth and speak loudly and clearly in a place that is quiet.

NOTE: If the voice memo system language does not match the language you are speaking, the device will not recognize your voice. Before you use this feature, click the current language to set the voice memo system language.

My Files

Access and manage different files stored in the device.

Open the **My Files** app.

To search for unnecessary data and free up your device's storage, click **Analyze storage**. To search for files or folders, click Q.

Gaming Hub

Gaming Hub collects your games downloaded from **Play Store** and **Galaxy Store** into one place for seamless access. You are able to set the device to game mode to play games more easily.

Open the **Gaming Hub** app and choose the game you want.

NOTE:

- If **Gaming Hub** does not show, launch the **Settings** app, click **Advanced features**, and then click the **Gaming Hub** switch to activate it.
- Games downloaded from **Play Store** and **Galaxy Store** automatically show on the Gaming Hub screen. If you cannot see your games, pull the Library panel upwards and click ⋮→**Add games**.

Removing a game from Gaming Hub

Go to **My games,** touch and hold the game you want to remove, and then click **Remove**.

Changing the performance mode

You can change the game performance mode.

Open the **Gaming Hub** app, tap **More** → **Game Booster** → **Game optimization**, and then choose the mode you want.

- **Performance**: This focuses on providing you with the best possible performance while playing games.

- **Standard**: This helps to balance the performance and the battery usage time.

- **Battery saver**: This will help you save battery power while playing games.

NOTE: Efficiency of battery power may vary depending on the game.

Game Booster

Game Booster allows you to play games in a better environment. You can use Game Booster while playing games.

To open the Game Booster panel while playing games, click ⚽ on the navigation bar. If the navigation bar does not show, drag upwards from the bottom of the screen to show it. If the navigation bar is set to use **Swipe gestures**, open the notification panel and click **Tap to open Game Booster.**

- ⚙ : Configure settings for Game Booster.

- ⊙ : Use this to lock the touch screen while playing game. To unlock, touch the screen and drag the lock icon in any direction on the screen.

- ⊙ : This feature hides buttons on the navigation bar. You can bring up the buttons again on the screen by tapping ⊟ on the navigation bar.

- ⊙ : Take screenshots.

- ⊙ : For recording your game sessions. Tap ■ to stop recording.

- **Priority mode**: Set the device to block incoming calls and all notifications except for alarms so as to prevent any disturbance when playing your game.

- **Monitoring temperature / Monitoring memory**: Configure the device to automatically adjust settings to prevent overheating and to stop apps running in the background to better manage your device's memory.

- **Navigation button lock**: Hide the buttons on the navigation bar away from view. To display the buttons, click⊟ on the navigation bar.

- **Screen touch lock**: Lock the touch screen while playing game. To unlock the touch screen, simply drag the lock icon in any direction.
- **Screenshot**: Capture screenshots.

NOTE:
- You can set to open the Game Booster panel from the navigation bar when the navigation bar is set to **Swipe gestures**. On the Game Booster panel, click ⚙ →**Block during game** and click the **Navigation gestures** switch to activate the feature.
- The options available may vary depending on the game.

Launching apps in pop-up windows while playing games

You can launch apps in pop-up windows even while playing a game.

Click ⚙ and select an app from the apps list.

Google apps

Google offers entertainment, social network, and business apps. You may need to have a Google account to access some apps.

To view more information about each app and access its help menu:

- **Chrome**: Search for information and browse web pages.

- **Gmail**: Sending or receiving emails via the Google Mail service.

- **Maps**: Find your exact location on the map, search the world map, and view information about you location and different places around you.

- **YT Music**: Enjoy yourself with different music and videos from YouTube Music. You can also view the music collections saved on your device and play them.

- **Play Movies & TV**: Purchase or rent videos, e.g. movies and TV programs, from **Play Store**.

- **Drive**: Store your content on the cloud, access it from anywhere and anytime, and share it with others.

- **YouTube**: Watch or create your own videos and share them with others.

- **Photos**: Search for, manage, and edit all your pictures and videos from different sources in one location.

- **Google**: Browse items on the Internet or your device.

- **Duo**: Make a simple video call.
- **Messages**: Send and receive messages on your device or computer, and share different types of content, e.g. images and videos.

NOTE: You may not find some apps, depending on the service provider or model.

CHAPTER 7
CONNECTIVITY AND SHARING

Wi-Fi

Activate the Wi-Fi feature to connect your device to a Wi-Fi network and be able to access the **Internet** or other network devices.

Connecting to a Wi-Fi network

1 On the Settings screen, click **Connections** → **Wi-Fi** and touch the switch to activate the feature.

2 Choose a network from the Wi-Fi networks list.

Networks with a lock icon means you need a password to connect to them.

NOTE:

- After the device has successfully connected to a Wi-Fi network for the first time, the device will reconnect to that network any other time it is available without requiring a password. To prevent the device from connecting to the network automatically, click ⚙ next to the network and click the **Auto reconnect** switch to deactivate it.

- If you're finding difficulty connecting to a Wi-Fi network properly, restart your device's Wi-Fi feature or the wireless router.

How to check the Wi-Fi network quality information

View the Wi-Fi network quality information, e.g. the speed and stability.

On the Settings screen, click **Connections** → **Wi-Fi** and click the switch to activate it. The network quality information will display under the Wi-Fi networks. If it does not display, click ⋮→**Intelligent Wi-Fi** and click the **Show network quality info** switch to activate it.

NOTE:The quality information may not show depending on the Wi-Fi network.

Sharing Wi-Fi network passwords

If you make a request to someone who is connected to a secured Wi-Fi network to share its password, you can connect to the network without entering the password. This feature is available between the devices which have contacts with each other and the you must ensure the screen of the other device is turned on.

1. On the Settings screen, click **Connections** → **Wi-Fi** and click the switch to activate it.
1. Choose a network from the Wi-Fi networks list.

2   Click on **Request password**.

3   Accept the share request on the other device.

    The Wi-Fi password is automatically entered on your device and will be connected to the network.

Wi-Fi Direct

Wi-Fi Direct connects devices directly via a Wi-Fi network without needing an access point.

1   On the Settings screen, click **Connections** → **Wi-Fi** and click the switch to activate it.

2   Click ⋮ → **Wi-Fi Direct**.

    The list of detected devices is displayed.

    If the device you want to connect to is not shown on the list, request that the device turns on its Wi-Fi Direct feature.

3   Choose a device to connect to.

    The devices will be connected when the other device accepts the request for Wi-Fi Direct connection.

    To terminate the device connection, select the device to disconnect from the list.

Bluetooth

Use Bluetooth for exchange of data or media files with other Bluetooth-enabled devices.

CAUTION:

- Samsung is not accountable for the loss, interception, or misuse of data sent or received via Bluetooth.
- Always make sure that you share and receive data with devices that are trusted and properly secured. If there are impediments between the devices, the operating distance may be reduced.
- Some devices may not be compatible with your device, especially those that are not tested or approved by the Bluetooth SIG.
- Never use the Bluetooth feature for illegal purposes (for example, pirating copies of files or illegally tapping communications for commercial purposes). Samsung will not take responsibility for the repercussion of illegal use of the Bluetooth feature.

How to pair your Galaxy A55 5G with other Bluetooth devices

1. On the **Settings** screen, click **Connections** → **Bluetooth** and click the switch to activate it. A list of the detected devices will pop up.
2. Choose a device to pair with.
   If the device you want to pair with is not displayed on the list, then set the device to enter Bluetooth pairing

mode. Refer to the other user manual of the other device.

NOTE: Your device will be visible to other devices while the Bluetooth settings screen is open.

3 Accept the Bluetooth connection request on your device to establish the connection.

The devices become connected when the other device accepts the Bluetooth connection request.

To unpair the devices, click ⚙ next to the device name and click **Unpair**.

Sending and receiving data

Several apps support data transfer via Bluetooth. You are able to share data, such as contacts or media files, with other Bluetooth devices. The underlisted actions are an example of sending an image to another device.

1 Open the **Gallery** app and choose an image.
2 Tap ⚆ → **Bluetooth** and choose a device to transfer the image to.

If the device you want to pair with is not in the list, request the device to turn on its visibility option.

3 Accept the request for Bluetooth connection on the other device.

NFC and contactless payments

Your device lets you read near field communication (NFC) tags that have information about products. You can also use this feature to make business transactions and purchase tickets for transportation or events after you have downloaded the relevant apps.

CAUTION: Your device contains a built-in NFC antenna. Handle the device with care to avoid damaging the NFC antenna.

Reading information from NFC tags

Make use of the NFC feature to read product information from NFC tags.

1 On the Settings screen, click **Connections** and click the **NFC and contactless payments** switch to activate it.
2 Place the NFC antenna area on the back of your device close to an NFC tag. The information from the tag will display.

NOTE: Make sure the device's screen is turned on and unlocked. If not, the device will not read NFC tags or receive data.

Making payments with the NFC feature

Before you can use the NFC feature to make payments, you must first of all register for the mobile payment service. If you want to register or get more information about the service, contact your service provider.

1   From the **Settings** screen, click **Connections** and click the **NFC and contactless payments** switch to activate the feature.
2   Use the NFC antenna area on the back of your device to touch the NFC card reader.

To set the default payment app, open the Settings screen and click **Connections** → **NFC and contactless pay-**

ments → **Contactless payments** → **Payment**, and then choose the app you want.

NOTE:

- All available payment apps may not be included in the payment services list.
- If you upgrade the payment app that you have been using or install a new one, it is possible that the payment services that you have been using in the past will no longer function properly. If this is the case, navigate to the **Settings** screen and choose **Connections**, followed by **NFC and contactless payments**, and then **Contactless payments** > **Payment** or **Others**, and then choose an alternative app to use instead of the one that was just updated or installed. Alternatively, deselect the app that has been chosen.

Data saver

Minimize your data usage by preventing some apps running in the background from sending or receiving data.

On the Settings screen, click **Connections** → **Data usage** → **Data saver** and click the switch to activate it.

When the data saver feature is activated, the icon will display on the status bar.

Data saver feature activated

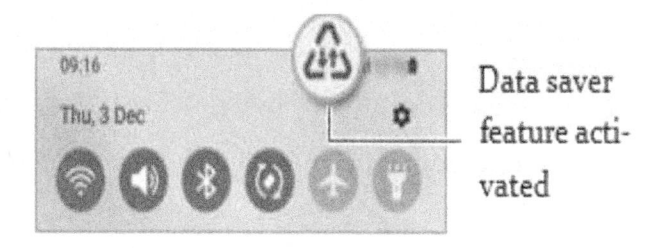

To select apps to use data without restriction, click **Allowed to use data while Data saver is on** and select apps.

Allowed network for apps

Choose apps to always use the mobile data or Wi-Fi network, or both.

For instance, you can set the device to use only mobile data for apps that you want to keep secure or streaming apps that can be disconnected. Even though you do not deactivate the Wi-Fi feature, the apps will start using the mobile data.

On the Settings screen, click **Connections → Data usage → Allowed network for apps**, tap the switch to activate it, and then tap the other switches next to the apps you want.

NOTE: You may incur extra charges when using this feature.

Mobile Hotspot

To use your device as a mobile hotspot to share your device's mobile data connection with other devices, follow these steps:

1. On the Settings screen, click **Connections → Mobile Hotspot and Tethering → Mobile Hotspot**.
2. Click the switch to activate it.
   The icon will show on the status bar.
   You can reconfigure the level of security and the password by tapping **Configure**.
3. On the other device's screen, search for your device from the Wi-Fi networks list and select it. Alternatively, click **QR code** on the mobile hotspot screen and scan the QR code with the other device.

NOTE:
- If you can't find the mobile hotspot on your device, click **Configure** and set **Band** to **2.4 GHz**, click **Advanced**, and then click the **Hidden network** switch to deactivate it.
- When you activate the **Auto Hotspot** feature, you can share your device's mobile data connection with other devices signed in to your Samsung account.

More connection settings

Personalize settings to control other connection features. From the Settings screen, click **Connections** → **More connection settings**.

- **Nearby device scanning**: Make the device to scan for nearby devices to connect to.

- **Printing**: Configure settings for printer plug-ins installed on your smartphone. You can search for available printers or add them manually to print files. Refer to Printing for further information.

- **VPN**: Set up virtual private networks (VPNs) on your smartphone to connect to a school or company's private network.

- **Private DNS**: Set your smartphone to use the security enhanced private DNS.

- **Ethernet**: As soon as you connect an Ethernet adaptor, you can use a wired network and configure network settings.

Printing

Configure settings for printer plug-ins installed on your smartphone. You can connect your smartphone to a printer via Wi-Fi or Wi-Fi Direct, and print images or documents.

NOTE: Some printers may not be compatible with your smartphone.

Adding printer plug-ins

Add printer plug-ins for the printers that you want to connect your device to.

1. From the Settings screen, click **Connections** → **More connection settings** → **Printing** → **Download plugin**.
2. Choose a printer plug-in and install it.
3. Choose the installed printer plug-in.

   Your smartphone will automatically search for printers that are connected to the same Wi-Fi network as itself.
4. Pick a printer to add.

NOTE: To add printers manually, click ⁝ → **Add printer**.

Printing content

While viewing content, such as images or documents, access the options list, click **Print**→ ▼ →**All printers...**, and then choose a printer.

NOTE: Printing methods may differ depending on the content type.

Different ways to share content on your Galaxy A55 5G smartphone

Share content by using different sharing options. The actions listed below are an example of sharing images.

1. Launch the **Gallery** app and choose an image.

2. Tap the **Share** icon and choose a sharing method you want.

NOTE: You may be charged extra when sharing files via the mobile network.

How to use the Quick Share

Sharing content with nearby devices

Share content with nearby devices using Wi-Fi Direct or Bluetooth, or with SmartThings supported devices.

1 Launch the **Gallery** app and choose an image.

2 On the other device, open the notification panel, swipe downwards, and then click (**Quick Share**) to activate the feature. If you don't find it there, click the Edits button and select **Edit,** and then drag it over to add it.

3 Tap the Share icon → **Quick Share** and choose a device to transfer the image to.

4 Accept the request to transfer file on the other device.

NOTE: This feature is not supported when sharing videos with TVs or SmartThings supported devices. If you like watching videos on TV, then use the Smart View feature.

Sharing content with your contacts

With this method, you're able to share content with people saved in your contacts.

Step 1: Open the **Gallery** app and select the image you want to share.

Step 2: Click the **Share** button ⁂, select **Quick Share**, and then select **View contact.**

Step 3: Select the contact you want to share with from your **Contacts** list.

How to use private sharing

With private sharing, you can share encrypted content with others and the recipients won't be able to save, copy, or resend such contents. This is a great way to share classified or confidential files.

To use private sharing, follow these steps:

Step 1
- Open the **Gallery** app and select an image you want to share.

Step 2
- Tap the **Share** icon and select **Quick Share**.
- Tap the **More options** icon and tap **Turn on Private sharing**.

Step 3
- Select the device you want to transfer the image to, or if its someone in your **Contacts**, tap **View contact**, and then select the contact.

Key: Share icon = ◅   More options = ⋮

Setting who can find your device

Determine who is allowed to find and send content to your device.

1. Open the notification panel, swipe downwards, and then click ⊙ (**Quick Share**) to activate the feature. You can also swipe down with two fingers from the Home screen and then click the **Quick Share** icon. The Quick Share settings screen will be displayed.
2. Choose an option.

- **Non one**: Don't allow other people to find your device.
- **Contacts only**: Allow only those in your contacts to share with your device.

- **Anyone nearby**: Allow any neighboring devices to share with your device.

Web link Sharing

Share large files by uploading files to the Samsung storage server and sharing them with others via a Web link.

1. Launch the **Gallery** app and choose an image.
2. Tap the **Share** icon ⌘, then tap **Quick Share**.
   The link for the image will be generated.
3. Choose a sharing option under the **Share to any device** section. Available options are:
   - **Copy link:** Share the link that has been copied to the clipboard
   - **Share link using app:** Select an app to share the link.
   - **Share using QR code:** Use the QR code generated to share the link.

Music Share

The Music Share feature offers you the liberty to share your Bluetooth speaker that is already connected to your device with another person. You can also listen to the same music on your Galaxy Buds and someone else's Galaxy Buds.

You can get this feature only on devices that support the Music Share feature.

How to share your Bluetooth speaker with another device

You will be able to listen to music on your smartphone and someone else's smartphone via your Bluetooth speaker.

1. Ensure that your smartphone and your Bluetooth speaker are connected.
2. Go to **Settings** on your phone and tap **Connected devices**, then turn on the **Music Share** switch by tapping on it.

    You can explore more features, such as setting who to share your device with, by tapping **Music Share**.
3. On your friend's smartphone, choose your speaker from the list of the Bluetooth devices.
4. On your Galaxy A55 5G smartphone, accept the request for connection. When you do that, your speaker will be shared.

    When you play music via your friend's smartphone, the music playing via your smartphone will automatically be paused.

Listening to music together with Galaxy Buds

You can listen to music on your smartphone together via your Buds and your friend's Buds.

This feature is supported only on the Galaxy Buds series devices.

1. Ensure that your smartphone and your Bluetooth speaker are connected.
2. Go to **Settings** on your phone and tap **Connected devices,** ant turn on the **Music Share** switch by tapping on it.

   You can explore more features, such as setting who to share your device with, by tapping **Music Share**.
3. On your Galaxy A55 5G smartphone, open the notification panel and select **Media output**.
4. Tap **Music Sare** and choose your friend's Buds from the detected devices list.
5. On your friend's smartphone, accept the request to connect.

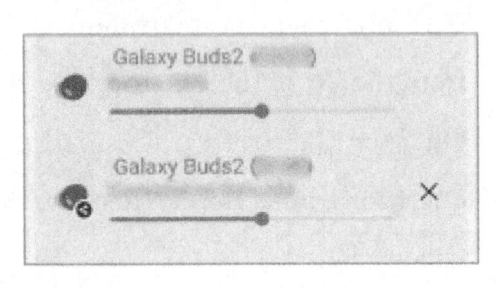

6. On your smartphone, mark your Buds and your friend's Buds on the audio output list.

When you play music via your smartphone, both of you can listen to it together through your buds and your friend's.

SmartThings

Take charge of and manage smart appliances and Internet of Things (IoT) products with your smartphone.

To find more information, launch the **SmartThings** app and click the **Menu** tab ≡→**How to use**.

1. Launch the **SmartThings** app.
2. Tap **Devices**→✛ or tap **Add device**
3. Choose a device and connect to it by following the on-screen instructions.

NOTE:

- Connection methods may vary according to the type of connected devices or the shared content.
- The devices you can connect vary by region. Available features may not be the same, depending on the connected device.

Connected devices' own errors or defects are not included in the Samsung warranty. If there are errors or defects on the connected devices, contact the device's manufacturer.

Smart View

View the content displayed on your device on a large screen by connecting your device to a screen mirroring-enabled TV or monitor.

1. Open the notification panel and swipe down, then click **Smart View**.
2. Choose a device to mirror your device's screen or display content.

NOTE: When you play a video with Smart View, the resolution may change depending on the TV model.

Link to Windows

You can connect your device to a Windows PC to quickly access your device's data, such as pictures or messages, on the computer.

When you have incoming calls or messages, you can receive them on the computer.

NOTE:

- This feature can only be found on Windows 10 version 1803 or higher, and it is recommended to use the latest Windows version and the **Phone Link** app to optimize this feature.

- You need to have a Microsoft account in order to use this feature. When you create a Microsoft account, you can sign in to access all Microsoft devices and services, such as Microsoft Office programs and Windows 10.

Connecting to a computer

1. Open the **Settings** app and click **Connected devices** → **Link to Windows**.
2. Follow the on-screen instructions to finish the connection.

How to view data and notifications from your smartphone on the computer

Open the **Phone Link** app on the computer and choose a category you want.

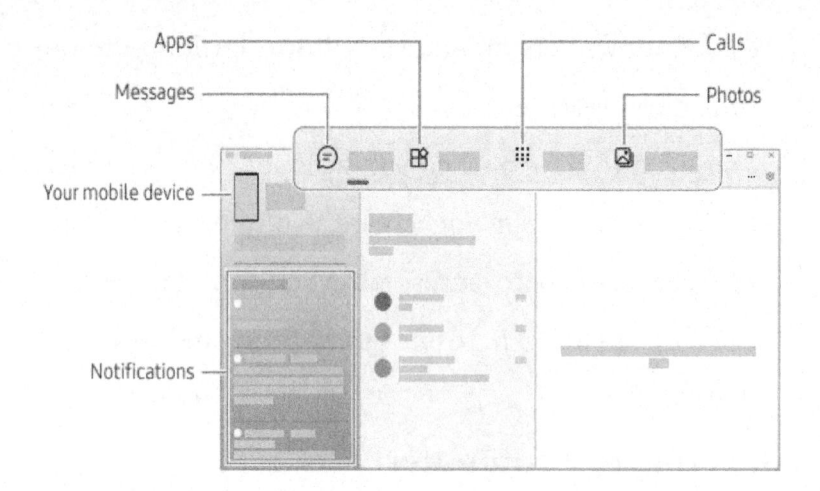

NOTE: Available features and menus may differ depending on the software version or model.

CHAPTER 8

CUSTOMIZATION SETTINGS

Customize your smartphone to your needs by modifying its settings.

To access the settings, go to the Apps screen. The alternative is to pull down the notification panel and click the Settings icon ⚙.

Use the **Search** button 🔍 to search for the settings you need by entering relevant keywords. In addition, you can look for settings by selecting a tag from the Suggestions menu.

Samsung account

Sign in to your Samsung account and manage it as desired.

On the Settings screen, click **Samsung account**.

Notifications

Change the notification settings.

On the Settings screen, click **Notifications**.

- **Notification pop-up style**: Choose a notification pop-up style and change the settings.

- **Do not disturb**: Configure your smartphone to mute all sounds apart from the allowed exceptions.

- **Advanced settings**: Configure advanced settings for notifications.

Display settings

Change the display and the Home screen settings.

On the Settings screen, click **Display**.

- **Light / Dark**: Activate or deactivate the dark mode feature.
- **Dark mode settings**: Reduce strain on your eye by applying the dark theme whenever you're using the device at night or in a dark place. You can set a schedule for when to apply dark mode.

NOTE:

The dark theme may not work in some apps.

- **Brightness**: Regulate the brightness of the display.
- **Adaptive brightness**: Make the device to keep up to date with your brightness adjustments and apply them automatically in similar lighting conditions.
- **Motion smoothness**: Modify the refresh rate of the screen. When you set high refresh rate, the screen will scroll more smoothly and seamlessly. Refer to Motion smoothness for further information.

- **Eye comfort shield**: Reduce eye strain by reducing the amount of blue light that is emitted by the screen. You can set a plan for applying this feature.
- **Screen mode**: Change the screen mode to regulate the display's color and contrast. Refer to Changing the screen mode or adjusting the display color for further information.
- **Font size and style**: Modify the font size and style.
- **Screen zoom**: Make the items on the screen bigger or smaller.
- **Full screen apps**: Choose apps to use with the full screen aspect ratio.
- **Screen timeout**: Set how long the device waits before turning off the display's backlight.
- **Easy mode**: Switch to easy mode to show larger icons and apply a simpler layout to the Home screen.
- **Edge panels**: Modify the settings for the Edge panel.
- **Navigation bar**: Change the navigation bar settings. Refer to Navigation bar (soft buttons) for further information.
- **Accidental touch protection**: Make the device's screen not detect any touch input when it is in a dark place, such as a pocket or bag.

- **Touch sensitivity**: Increase the touch sensitivity of the screen when used with screen protectors.
- **Show charging information**: Set the device to show the charging information, such as the remaining battery percentage when the screen is off.
- **Screen saver**: Set the device to start a screen saver when the device is charging.

NOTE: Some features may not be found depending on the model.

Motion smoothness

The refresh rate refers to the number of times the screen is refreshed every second. Use a high refresh rate so that the screen does not glimmer when switching between screens. The screen will scroll more smoothly. Your battery usage will reduce when you select a standard refresh rate, meaning you can use the battery longer.

1. On the Settings screen, click **Display** → **Motion smoothness**.
2. Choose a refresh rate.
    - **Adaptive**: Experience a smooth animation and scrolling by automatically regulating your screen refresh rate up to 120 Hz.

- **Standard**: Use a standard refresh rate in normal situations to reduce battery power consumption.

How to change the screen mode or adjust the display color:

Change the screen mode or adjust the display color to your favorite.

Changing the screen mode
On the Settings screen, click **Display** → **Screen mode** and choose a mode you want.

- **Vivid**: This enhances the color range, saturation, as well as the sharpness of your display. You can also alter the display color balance by color value.
- **Natural**: This alters the screen to a natural tone.

NOTE: You cannot adjust the display color except in **Vivid** mode.

- **Vivid** mode may not function well with third-party apps.

Optimizing the full screen color balance
improve the display color by adjusting the color tones to your own preference. On the Settings screen, click **Display** → **Screen mode** → **Vivid** and fine-tune the color adjustment bar under **White balance**.

When you pull the color adjustment bar towards **Cool**, the blue color tone will increase. When you pull the bar towards **Warm**, the red color tone will increase.

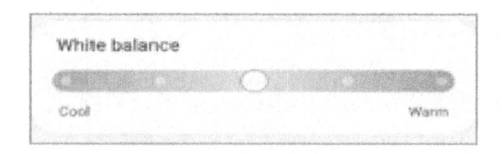

Adjusting the screen tone by color value

Increase or lower certain color tones by modifying the Red, Green, or Blue value individually.

1. On the Settings screen, click **Display** → **Screen mode** → **Vivid**.
2. Tap **Advanced settings**.
3. Adjust the **R** (Red), **G** (Green), or **B** (Blue) color bar as desired. The screen tone will be adjusted.

Wallpaper

Change the wallpaper settings for the Home screen and the locked screen. Once in **Settings**, click **Wallpaper and style**.

Themes

Apply different themes to your smartphone to change the visual elements of the Home screen, locked screen, and icons. From the **Settings** screen menu, click **Themes**.

CHAPTER 9
SETTINGS (PART 2)

Home screen

Configure your personal settings for the Home screen, such as the screen layout.

Open the **Settings** screen menu, click **Home screen**.

Lock screen

Options

Modify the settings for the locked screen.

On the Settings screen, click **Lock screen**.

- **Screen lock type**: Modify the screen lock method.
- **Smart Lock**: Make the device to unlock itself when trusted locations or devices are detected. Refer to Smart Lock for further information.
- **Secure lock settings**: Modify screen lock settings for the chosen lock method.
- **Always On Display**: Set the device to display information while the screen is turned off. See Always On Display for more information.
- **Wallpaper services**: Make the device to utilize wallpaper services such as Dynamic Lock screen.

- **Clock style**: Modify the type and color of the clock on the locked screen.
- **Roaming clock**: Alternate the clock to show both the local and home time zones on the locked screen when roaming.
- **Widgets**: Change the settings of the items that are displayed on the locked screen.
- **Contact information**: Make the device to show contact information, such as your email address, on the locked screen.
- **Notifications**: Set how notifications should show on the locked screen.
- **Shortcuts**: Choose apps to display shortcuts to them on the locked screen.
- **About Lock screen**: Take a look at the Lock screen version and legal information.

NOTE:The available options may be different depending on the screen lock method you have chosen.

Extended Unlock

This feature (also referred to as Smart Lock) allows you to configure your Galaxy A55 5G to unlock itself and stay unlocked when trusted locations or devices are detected.

For example, if you have set your home or office as a trusted location, whenever you get home or to your office, your device will detect the location and automatically unlock itself.

From the **Settings** screen, click **Lock screen** → **Extended Unlock** and follow the on-screen instructions to finish the setup.

NOTE:

- You will be able to use this feature only after you have set a screen lock method.
- If you have not used your device for at least four hours or when you turn it on, you must have to unlock the screen by using the pattern, PIN, or password you set.

Always On Display

You can view some information, such as the clock or calendar, or control music playback on the screen when it is turned off.

You can also find out about notifications for new messages or missed calls.

The Always On Display is set to appear only when you tap the screen. To change the settings to make it display non-stop or during a set time, go to the **Settings** menu, click

Lock screen → Always On Display → When to show, and then choose a mode you want.

NOTE: The brightness of the Always On Display may change any time automatically based on the lighting conditions.

Opening notifications on the Always On Display

When you receive message, missed call, or app notifications, notification icons will show on the Always On Display. Double-click a notification icon to view its notification.

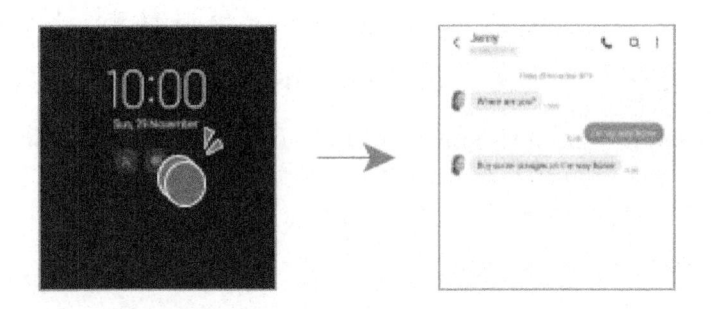

NOTE: If the screen is locked, you must first of all unlock it to view notifications.

Deactivating the Always On Display feature

Open the notification panel, swipe down, and then click the **Always On Display** icon to deactivate it. If you don't find it on the quick settings panel, open the **Edits menu** and drag the button over to add it.

Alternatively, from the Settings menu, click **Lock screen and AOD**, and then push the **Always On Display** switch off.

Security and privacy
Options

Modify the settings for securing your device.

On the Settings screen, click **security and privacy**.

- **Face recognition**: Set your smartphone to unlock the screen by recognizing your face. Refer to *Face recognition* for detailed information.
- **Fingerprints**: Register your fingerprints for you to unlock the screen. Refer to *Fingerprint recognition* for additional information.
- **Auto Blocker**: Keep your phone sage by blocking threats and other suspicious activity.
- **Account Security**: Make changes to your account settings.
- **App security**: Scan apps and keep your phone safe from malicious software.
- **More privacy settings**: Modify the settings for biometric data. You can also view the version of the biometrics security patch and check for updates.

- **Google Play Protect**: Make the device to check for harmful apps and behavior and warn about potential harm and remove them.
- **Security update**: Ascertain the version of your device's software and check for updates.
- **Lost device protection**: Activate or deactivate the feature for Find My Mobile. Access the Find My Mobile website (findmymobile.samsung.com) to track and control your device if it gets lost or stolen.
- **Samsung Pass**: Verify your identity easily and safely through your biometric data. Refer to *Samsung Pass* for additional information.
- **Secure Folder**: Create a secure folder to help you protect your private content and apps from others.
- **Secure Wi-Fi**: Configure the device to protect your data any time you're using unsecured Wi-Fi networks.
- **Private Share**: Share files with others through a secure means using blockchain technology.
- **Samsung Blockchain Keystore**: Manage your blockchain private key safely.
- **Permission manager**: Allow or disallow apps to access features or data on your phone.

- **Encrypt SD card**: Set your device to encrypt files on a memory card.

CAUTION:

If you have this setting enabled in your device when you reset your device to the factory defaults, the device will not be able to read your encrypted files. You must first of all disable this setting before resetting the device.

- **Other security settings**: Configure additional security settings.

NOTE: You may not find some features available depending on the service provider or model.

Secure Folder

Secure Folder helps you to secure your private content and apps, such as pictures and contacts, from being accessed by others even when the device is unlocked.

CAUTION:

Secure Folder is a distinct, secured storage area. You cannot transfer the data in Secure Folder to other devices by means of unauthorized sharing methods, such as USB or Wi-Fi Direct. Any attempt to personalize the operating system or modifying software will cause Secure Folder to be automatically locked and inaccessible. Before saving data in Secure Folder, be sure you have a backup copy of the data in another secure location.

How to Set up Secure Folder

1. Open the **Settings** app and click **Security and privacy** > **More security settings** > **Secure Folder**.
2. Complete the setup by following the on-screen instructions.

   Tap **Turn on** when a pop-up window requesting that you reset the Secure Folder lock type using your Samsung account appears. Using your Samsung account, you can reset the lock type if you've forgotten it. You won't be able to reset the lock type if you don't activate this feature after you forget it.

   The Secure Folder screen will display and the Secure Folder app icon (▣) will be added to the Apps screen. To change the name or icon color of Secure Folder, click ⋮ and go to **Customize**.

NOTE:

- When you start the **Secure Folder** app, you'll have to unlock the app using your preset lock technique.

- To change the name or icon of the Secure Folder, tap ⋮ and select **Customize**.

- If you forget your Secure Folder unlock code, you will not be able to reset it using your Samsung account. Click the button at the bottom of the locked screen, and input your Samsung account password.

Setting an auto lock condition for Secure Folder

1 Open the **Secure Folder** app and click ⋮ → **Settings** → **Auto lock Secure Folder**.

2 Choose a lock option.

NOTE: To manually lock your Secure Folder, click ⋮ → **Lock and exit**.

How to Move content to Secure Folder

Transfer content, such as pictures and videos, to Secure Folder. The following procedures are an example of moving an image from the default storage to Secure Folder.

1 Start the **Secure Folder** app and click ⋮ → **Add files**.

2 Click **Images**, tick images to move, and then click **Done**.

3 Click **Move**.

The ticked items will be deleted from the original folder and moved to Secure Folder. To copy items, click **Copy**.

NOTE: The method for moving content may not be the same, depending on the content type.

Moving content from Secure Folder

Transfer files from the Secure Folder to the appropriate app in the default storage location. The following steps will show you how to transfer a picture from the Secure Folder to the default storage location.

1. Launch the **Secure Folder** app and navigate to the **Gallery** menu option.
2. Select the image to move, tap ⋮ and then hit the button labeled "**Move out of Secure Folder**."
3. The objects that you have chosen will have their default storage location changed to the **Gallery** folder.

Adding apps

Add an app to use in Secure Folder.

1. Start the **Secure Folder** app and tap ✚.
2. Choose one or more apps installed on your phone and click **Add**.

Removing apps from Secure Folder

Click and hold an app to delete, and click **Uninstall**.

Adding accounts

Add any of your accounts, like Samsung and Google accounts, or other accounts, to sync with the apps in Secure Folder.

1. Launch the **Secure Folder** app and click ⋮ → **Settings** → **Manage accounts** → **Add account**.
2. Choose an account service.
3. Complete the account setup by following the on-screen instructions.

Hiding Secure Folder

You will be able to hide the Secure Folder shortcut, if you like, from the Apps screen.

Launch the **Secure Folder** app, tap ⋮→**Settings**, and then click **Add Secure Folder to Apps screen** and turn off the switch.

Alternatively, open the notification panel, swipe down, and then click 🔲 (**Secure Folder**) to deactivate the feature.

If you can't find it there, tap the **Add** button and drag it over to include it.

If you want the Secure Folder to be visible again, start the **Settings** app, click **Security and privacy** > **Biometrics** > **Secure Folder**, and then click the **Add Secure folder to Apps screen** switch to activate it.

Uninstalling Secure Folder

If you wish to, you can uninstall Secure Folder, including the content and apps in it any time.

Open the **Secure Folder** app and click **⋮** → **Setting** → **More settings** → **Uninstall**.

If you want to back up your files before uninstalling Secure Folder, tick **Move media files out of Secure Folder** and select the **Uninstall** option. To access data you have backed up from Secure Folder, open the **My Files** app and click **Internal storage,** go to **Download,** and then **Secure Folder**.

NOTE: Notes saved in **Samsung Notes** is not going to have a backup.

Secure Wi-Fi

Secure Wi-Fi is a service that secures your Wi-Fi network connection. It encrypts data by using Wi-Fi networks and also disables tracking apps and websites in a way that you can use Wi-Fi networks securely.

For example, when using an unsecure Wi-Fi network in public places, such as cafes or airports, Secure Wi-Fi is automatically activated in a manner that no one will be able to hack your login information or watch your activity in apps and websites.

From the **Settings** menu, select **Security and privacy,** select **More Security settings,** then select **Secure Wi-Fi** and follow the on-screen instructions to complete the setup.

When you activate the Secure Wi-Fi, the Wi-Fi 🛡 icon will be displayed on the status bar.

NOTE:

- Using this feature may result in a decreased Wi-Fi network speed.

- This feature may not be available depending on the Wi-Fi network, service provider, or model.

How to select the apps to protect using Secure Wi-Fi

You can select the apps you want to protect using Secure Wi-Fi in order to safely protect data, such as your password or your activity in apps, from being accessed by anyone else.

From the Settings screen, click **Security and privacy** > **More security settings** > **Secure Wi-Fi**. Then tap the **More options** tab (⋮) on the top right corner) and go to **Settings** > **Protected apps** and click the switches next to the apps you want to protect using Secure Wi-Fi.

NOTE: Some apps may not support this feature.

How to purchase a protection plan

You are given a free protection plan for Wi-Fi networks each month. But you can as well purchase paid protection plans and get unlimited bandwidth protection for a restricted time.

1. From the Settings screen, click **Security and privacy** > **More security settings** > **Secure Wi-Fi**.
2. Select the **Protection plan** and **Upgrade** options from their respective menus, and then choose the plan you want.

    NOTE: For some kind of protection plans, you can transfer the protection plan to another device signed in to your Samsung account.
3. Complete the purchase by following the on-screen instructions.

CHAPTER 10
MODES AND ROUTINES ON THE GALAXY A55 5G

You may use your device in a more convenient manner by selecting a mode that corresponds to your present activity or location, or you can add your routines that correspond to your typical patterns of use.

To access **Modes and Routines**, open the **Settings** screen's menu.

Adding modes

1. To add modes, open the **Settings** screen menu and select **Modes and Routines**.

2. Choose the mode that you wish to use, or hit the **Add mode** button to create your own modes.

Running modes

When the conditions for a mode are recognized, that mode will begin to run automatically. You may also choose to operate them manually by pressing the button at the appropriate time.

To manually run a mode, choose the mode you wish to run and then hit the **Turn on** button.

To disable a mode that is currently active, tap the mode, and then hit the **Turn off** button.

Adding new routines

1. Open the **Settings** screen and tap **Modes and Routines,** then select **Routines.**

2. You may tap ⊘ to choose a routine that interests you, or you can tap the **Add** button ✛ to create your own routines.

Tap "**Start manually**" if you wish to make the manual running condition the default for the routine. This option will only be accessible in the absence of any predefined running conditions. Tap the **Add** button when the pop-up window displays. You have the option of adding the routine as a widget to the Home screen, from which you can then easily access it.

Running routines

Whenever a predefined set of conditions is met, the associated auto routines will be performed. If you specify the running condition of a routine to be the **Start manually**, then you'll be able to execute that routine manually by clicking on the button at any time you want.

Tap the **Start** ▶ button next to the routine if you wish to execute manually, and then follow the on-screen prompts. You may also select the widget that represents the routine from the Home screen.

To stop running routines, select the routine in the **Running** section and press **Stop**.

Sounds and vibration

Options

Change settings for different sounds on the device.

On the Settings screen, clicks **Sounds and vibration**.

- **Sound mode**: Make the device to use sound mode, vibration mode, or silent mode.

- **Vibrate while ringing**: Make the device to vibrate and play a ringtone for incoming calls.

- **Temporary mute**: Make the device to use silent mode for a certain period.

- **Ringtone**: Change the call ringtone.

- **Notification sound**: Change the notification sound.

- **System sound**: Alter the sound to use for some kinds of actions, such as charging the device.

- **Volume**: Regulate the device's volume level.

- **Call vibration pattern**: Change the call vibration pattern.

- **Notification vibration pattern**: Change the notification vibration pattern.

- **Vibration intensity**: Regulate the force of the vibration notification.

- **System sound/vibration control**: Make the device to sound or vibrate for actions, such as controlling the touch screen.

- **Sound quality and effects**: Set the sound quality and effects of the device. Refer to Sound quality and effects for further information.

- **Separate app sound**: Make the device to play media sound from a specific app separately on the other audio device. Refer to Separate app sound for further information.

NOTE:Some features may be unavailable depending on the model.

Sound quality and effects

Set the device's sound quality and effects.

On the Settings screen, click **Sounds and vibration** → **Sound quality and effects**.

- **Dolby Atmos**: Choose a surround sound mode optimized for different types of audio, such as movies, music, and voice. Using Dolby Atmos, you can experience moving audio sounds that flow all around you.
- **Dolby Atmos for gaming**: Experience the Dolby Atmos sound optimized for games as you play games.
- **Equalizer**: Choose an option for a specific music genre and enjoy optimized sound.
- **UHQ upscaler**: Increase the sound resolution of music and videos.
- **Adapt sound**: Make the best sound for you.

NOTE: Subject to the model, you must connect an earphone to use some features.

Separate app sound

Make the device to play media sound from a specific app on the connected Bluetooth speaker or headset.

For example, you can listen to the Navigation app through your device's speaker while at the same time listening to playback from the Music app through the vehicle's Bluetooth speaker.

1. On the Settings screen, click **Sounds and vibration** → **Separate app sound** and click the switch to activate it.

2 Choose an app to play media sounds separately and click the Back button.

3 Choose a device for playing the chosen app's media sound.

CHAPTER 11
ACCOUNTS AND BACKUP

Sync, back up, or restore your smartphone's data using Samsung Cloud. You can also sign in to accounts, such as your Samsung account or Google account, or transfer data to or from other devices by using Smart Switch.

On the Settings screen, click **Accounts and backup**.

- **Manage accounts**: Add your Samsung and Google accounts, or other accounts, to sync with.
- **Samsung Cloud**: Back up your data and settings, and restore the previous device's data and settings even when you do not have it. Refer to Samsung Cloud for further information.
- **Google Drive**: Keep your personal information, app data, and settings safe on your smartphone. You can back up your sensitive information. You must have to sign in to your Google account to back up data.
- **Smart Switch**: Launch Smart Switch and transfer data from your old device. Refer to *Transferring data from your previous device (Smart Switch)* for additional information.

NOTE: Back up your data often to a safe location, such as Samsung Cloud or a computer, so that you can restore it if the data is corrupted or lost due to an accidental factory data reset.

Samsung Cloud

Back up your smartphone's data to Samsung Cloud and restore it later.

Backing up data to Samsung Cloud

You can back up your smartphone's data to Samsung Cloud.

1. From the Settings screen, click **Accounts and backup** and click **Back up data** under **Samsung Cloud**.
2. Mark items you want to back up and click **Back up now**.
3. Click the **Done** button.

NOTE:
- All of your data will not be backed up. To check which data will be backed up, on the Settings screen, click **Accounts and backup** > **Back up data** under the **Samsung Cloud** section.
- To check the backup data for other devices in your Samsung Cloud, navigate to the **Settings** screen, click

Accounts and backup → **Restore data**, and then choose a device you want.

Restoring data

You can restore your backup data from Samsung Cloud to your smartphone.

1 From the Settings screen, click **Accounts and backup**.
2 Click **Restore data** and choose a device you want.
3 Mark items you want to restore and click **Restore**.

CHAPTER 12
ADVANCED SETTINGS

Advanced features

Activate advanced features and modify the settings that control each feature.

From the Settings screen, click **Advanced features**.

- **Call & text on other devices**: Use your device's calling and messaging features on other devices that are signed in to your Samsung account.

- **Continue apps on other devices**: Use your device's apps on other devices that are signed in to your Samsung account.

- **Link to Windows**: Promptly access data saved in your device on your computer. See the section on *Link to Windows* for further details.

- **Android Auto**: Connect your device to a vehicle and control some of your device's features on the vehicle's display.

- **Side key**: Select an app or feature to start using the Side key. Refer to *Setting the Side key* for further information.

- **Motions and gestures**: Activate the motion feature and organize settings. Refer to *Motions and gestures* for additional information.

- **One-handed mode**: Activate one-handed operation mode for your convenience when using the smartphone with one hand.
- **Bixby Routines**: Add routines to automate settings that you use frequently. Your smartphone also recommends useful routines according to your frequent activities. Refer to *Bixby Routines* for additional information.
- **Screenshots and screen recorder**: Modify the settings for screenshots and screen recorder.
- **Show contacts when sharing content**: Make the device to display the people you contacted on the sharing options panel to let you share content directly.
- **Dual Messenger**: Install the second app. Use two distinct accounts for the same messenger app. Refer to *Dual Messenger* for more details.

NOTE: Some features may be unavailable depending on the service provider or model.

Motions and gestures

Activate the motion feature and configure settings.

From the Settings screen, click **Advanced features** → **Motions and gestures**.

- **Lift to wake**: Make the device to turn on the screen anytime you pick it up.
- **Double tap to turn on screen**: Make the device to turn on the screen by double-tapping anywhere on the screen while it's is turned off.

- **Double tap to turn off screen**: Make the device to turn off the screen when you double-tap an empty area on the Home screen or the locked screen.
- **Keep screen on while viewing**: Make the device to stop the display from turning off while you are looking at it.
- **Alert when phone picked up**: Make the device to prompt you if you have missed calls or new messages whenever you pick up the device.

    NOTE: This feature may not respond if the device's screen is turned on or the device is not placed on a flat surface.

- **Mute with gestures**: Make the device to mute some kind of sounds by using motions or gestures.
- **Palm swipe to capture**: Make the device to capture a screenshot when you swipe your hand to the left or right across the screen. You can view the captured images in your device's **Gallery**. Some apps and features will not allow you to capture a screenshot while using them.

NOTE: Excessive shaking or an impact to the device may cause an input that is not intended in situations of some features using sensors.

Video call effects

During video calls, you may use several options such as altering the background.

Press Advanced features, then Video call effects while on the Settings screen, then tap the switch to turn it on. The ⊙ icon will be placed to the screen of the video calling app.

Making use of video call effects

Tap ⊙ on the screen of the video calling app.

• Reset all: Reset all of the settings.

• Background: During video calls, change or blur the background.

• Auto framing: Turn on or off the feature of auto framing. When you enable this function, the device adjusts the filming angle and zoom automatically during video conversations by recognizing and tracking individuals.

• Settings: Choose from a variety of backdrop colors and graphics to use during video conversations.

NOTE:

• Depending on the model, some functionalities may be unavailable.

• Some functionalities are only available when the front camera is used.

Dual Messenger

Install another app and use two distinct accounts for the same messenger app.

1 From the Settings screen, click **Advanced features** → **Dual Messenger**.

 Supported apps will show.

2 Click the switch of an app to install the second app and you will have it installed. The second app's icon will be shown with ⊙.

— Second app

NOTE:

- Depending on the app, the Dual Messenger feature may not be available.
- The second app may have limited features.

Uninstalling a second app

1 From the Settings screen, click **Advanced features** → **Dual Messenger**.

2 Click the switch of the app you want to uninstall and click **Uninstall**. Every data relating to the second app will be deleted from the device.

NOTE: If the first app is uninstalled, the second app will also be deleted.

Digital Wellbeing and parental controls

View the history of your device usage and use features to stop your device from meddling with your life. You may also like to set up parental controls for your children and manage their digital use.

From the Settings screen, click **Digital Wellbeing and parental controls**.

- **Screen time**: Set goals for how much you use your device daily.
- **App timers**: Limit each app's daily usage time by setting a timer. When you get to the limit, the app will be deactivated and you will not be able to use it more.
- **Focus mode**: Activate focus mode. This helps you to avoid distractions from your device and stay focused on what you want. You can allow some apps to be used in focus mode.
- **Bedtime mode**: Activate bedtime mode to reduce eye strain before you go to sleep and prevent you from being disturbed while sleeping.
- **Parental controls**: Take charge of your children's digital use.

Battery and device care

The device care feature gives you a summary of the position of your device's battery, storage, memory, and system security. You are also able to automatically optimize the device by simply tapping with your finger.

Optimizing your device

From the Settings screen, click **Battery and device care** → **Optimize now**.

The quick optimization feature enhances the device performance through the following means:

- Helping to close apps that may be running in the background.
- Managing unusual battery usage.

- Scanning for any crashed apps and malware in your device.

How to use the auto optimization feature

Your device can be set to perform auto optimization when it is not in use. In **Settings,** click **Device care** > **Optimize now.** The quick optimization feature helps to enhance your device's performance through the following ways:

- By closing apps that are running in the background.
- By managing unusual battery usage.
- Scanning for crashed apps and malware.

Battery

Check the remaining battery power and how long you can use the device. If your devices have low battery level, conserve battery power by activating power saving features.

From the Settings screen, click **Device care** → **Battery**.

- **Power saving mode**: Activate power saving mode to lengthen the battery's usage time.

- **Background usage limits**: Limit battery usage for apps that you do not use frequently.

- **More battery settings**: Configure advanced battery settings.

NOTE:

- The usage time left shows how long more you can use the device before the battery power runs out. Usage time left may by device settings and operating conditions.

- You may not receive notifications from some apps when using power saving mode.

Storage

Check the status of the used memory as well as the available memory.

From the Settings screen, click **Device care** → **Storage**. To delete files or uninstall apps that you no longer use, choose a category. Then, click and hold, or choose, an item and click **Delete** or **Uninstall**.

NOTE:

- The actual available capacity of the internal memory is usually less than the stated capacity. This is because the operating system and default apps occupy part of the memory.

   The available capacity may change still anytime you update the device.

- To view the available capacity of the internal memory, access the Specification section for your device on the Samsung website.

Memory

From the Settings screen, click **Device care** → **Memory**.

To speed up your device by stopping apps running in the background, mark apps from the apps list, and click **Clean now**.

App protection

Check the security status of your device. This feature helps to scan your device for malware.

From the Settings screen, click **Device care** → **App protection** → **Scan phone**.

Maintenance mode

To maintain your privacy while another person is using your device, such as when you send it in for repairs, you should safeguard it by activating the maintenance mode.

You can activate maintenance mode from the **Settings** screen by selecting **Device care** > **Maintenance mode** > **Turn on**.

How to use the Ultra data saving mode

You may control and limit your mobile data consumption by blocking apps from accessing the connection when they are in the background. You may also compress internet data, such as photos, movies, and webpages, that you access over the mobile network by making use of the data compression tool.

To activate Ultra data saving, go to the **Settings** menu, then select **Device care** and toggle on the corresponding switch.

• This function might not be accessible depending on the mobile network you use or the device you purchase. When this function is activated, it is possible that certain web sites or content will not be accessible due to limitations imposed by the service provider or the constraints of the mobile network.

Apps

Manage the apps in your device and change their settings. You are able to view the apps' usage information, change their notification or permission settings, or uninstall or disable any unnecessary apps.

From the Settings screen, click **Apps**.

General management

Personalize your device's system settings or reset the device.

From the Settings screen, click **General management**.

- **Language**: Choose device languages. Refer to *Adding device languages* for more details.

- **Text-to-speech output**: Change the settings for text-to-speech features to make use of when you activate Talk-Back. For instance, you can modify languages, speed, and more.

- **Date and time**: Access and modify the settings to control how your device displays the time and date.

    NOTE:If the battery becomes completely discharged, the time and date is reset.

- **Samsung Keyboard settings**: Alter the settings for the Samsung keyboard.

- **Keyboard list and default**: Choose a keyboard to use by default and alter the keyboard settings.

- **Physical keyboard**: Alter the settings for an external keyboard.
- **Mouse and trackpad**: Alter the settings for an external mouse or trackpad.
- **Autofill service**: Choose an autofill service to use.
- **Reset**: Reset the settings of your device or execute a factory data reset.
- **Contact us**: Make an enquiry or view frequently asked questions.

Adding device languages

Add more languages to use on your device.

1 From your Settings screen, click **General management** → **Language** → **Add language**. If you like to view all the languages you can possibly add, click **⋮**→**All languages**.

2 Choose a language to add.

3 To set the chosen language as the default language, click **Set as default**. To retain the current language setting, click **Keep current**.

The chosen language will be added to your languages list. If you have modified the default language, the chosen language will be added to the top of the list.

To alter the default language from your languages list, choose the language you want and click**Apply**. If there's any app that doesn't support the default language, the next supported language in the list will be used instead.

Accessibility

Configure various settings in your device to improve its accessibility.

From the Settings screen, click **Accessibility**.

- **Recommended for you**: Find out about the accessibility features you are currently using and see other recommended features you may like.

- **TalkBack**: Activate TalkBack, which offers you voice feedback. To view help information to know more about how you can use this feature, click **Settings** → **TalkBack tutorial**.

- **Visibility enhancements**: Personalize the settings to improve accessibility for users with impaired vision.

- **Hearing enhancements**: Personalize the settings to enhance accessibility for users with hearing impairment.

- **Interaction and dexterity**: Personalize the settings to enhance accessibility for users who have low dexterity.

- **Advanced settings**: Configure settings concerning Direct access and notification features.

- **Installed services**: View accessibility services installed on your smartphone.

- **About Accessibility**: Take a look at the Accessibility information.

- **Contact us**: Make enquiry or view frequently asked questions.

Software update

Update the software of your smartphone through the firmware over-the-air (FOTA) service. You can also plan software updates.

From the Settings screen, click **Software update**.

- **Download and install**: Find out about updates and install them manually.
- **Auto download over Wi-Fi**: Make the device to download updates automatically whenever it's connected to a Wi-Fi network.
- **Last update**: Review information about the last software update.

NOTE:

Whenever there are emergency software updates which are meant to secure your device and to block new types of security threats, they will be installed automatically without your consent.

Security updates information

Security updates are meant to strengthen the security of your device and protect your personal information from external threats. For security updates for your device's model, visit *security.samsungmobile.com*.

NOTE: The website does not support all languages.

About phone

Access useful information about your device.

From the Settings screen, click **About phone**.

To modify your device's name, click **Edit**.

- **Status information**: Take a look at a number of device information, such as the SIM card status, Wi-Fi MAC address, and serial number.

- **Legal information**: Access legal information concerning the device, such as safety information and the opensource license.

- **Software information**: See the software information of your smartphone, such as the versions of its operating system and firmware.

- **Battery information**: Show the device's battery status and information.

CHAPTER 13
CARE AND MAINTENANCE TIPS

Precautions for using the device

Please take time to read this manual before using the device to guarantee safe and proper use.

- The descriptions used here are based on the device's default settings.

- Some of the content in your device may not be the same depending on your region or service provider. It may also vary by model specifications, or device's software.

- The device may need a connection to a Wi-Fi or mobile network when you are using some apps or features.

- Content (high quality content) that needs high CPU and RAM usage will inevitably affect the general performance of the device. Apps associated to the content may not work correctly depending on the device's specifications and the environment that it is used in.

- Samsung does not take legal responsibility for any performance problems that may be caused by apps gotten from other sources than Samsung.

- Samsung does not take legal responsibility for any performance problems or incompatibilities arising from edited registry settings or modified operating system software. Trying to customize the operating system may cause the device or apps to work inappropriately.

- Software, sound sources, wallpapers, images, and other media supplied with this device are licensed for restricted use. Extracting and using these materials for commercial or other purposes is a violation of copyright laws. Users are fully accountable for illegal use of media.

- You may have to pay extra charges for data services, such as messaging, uploading and downloading, auto-syncing, or using location services which are dependent on your existing data plan. For large data transfers, it is advisable to use the Wi-Fi feature.

- Default apps that come along with the device are liable to updates and may no longer be supported without previous notice. If you have queries about an app provided with the device, you can contact a Samsung Service Centre. For user-installed apps, contact your service providers.

- Modifying the device's operating system or installing software from unauthorized sources may cause the device to malfunction, result in data corruption or loss. These actions equate to violations of your Samsung license agreement and will render your warranty void.

- Depending on the region you live or your service provider, a screen protector is usually attached to your device for protection during production and distribution. Although, your warranty does not cover any damage to the screen protector.

- You'll be able see the touchscreen clearly even in strong outdoor sunlight by automatically adjusting the contrast range depending on the surrounding environment. Owing to the nature of the device, displaying fixed graphics for extended periods may cause afterimages (screen burn-in) or ghosting.

  — It is advisable not to use fixed graphics on part or all of the touchscreen for a long period and turn off the touchscreen when the device is not in use.

  — You can set the touchscreen to turn off automatically when it is not in using. From the **Settings** app, tap **Display** → **Screen timeout**, and then choose the length of time you want the device to wait before turning off the touchscreen.

  — If you want to set the touchscreen to automatically adjust its brightness based on the immediate environment, launch the **Settings** app, tap **Display**, and then tap the **Adaptive brightness** switch to activate it.

- Depending on the region or model, some devices may need authorization from the Federal Communications Commission (FCC).

  If your device is permitted by the FCC, you can view the FCC ID of the device. To see the FCC ID, go to the **Settings** app and launch, then tap **About phone** →

Status information. If your device does not have an FCC ID, it means that the device has not been approved for sale in the U.S. or its territories. In that case, it may only be brought to the U.S. for the owner's personal use.

- The use of mobile devices on airplanes or ships depend on applicable federal and local guidelines and restrictions. Find out from appropriate authorities and always follow crew instructions about when and how you may use your device.

- You can view the regulatory information on the device depending on your region. To see the information, open the **Settings** app and click **About phone** → **Regulatory information**.

- Please note that your device has magnets. You are therefore advised to keep it safely from objects that may have any interference with magnets such as credit cards and implantable medical devices. If you have an implantable medical device, you're advised to consult your physician before using this device.

Maintaining water and dust resistance

Your device is water- and dust-resistant. Ensure you follow these tips cautiously to preserve the water- and dust-resistance of your device. Failure to do so may lead to damage of your device.

- Do not dip the device in fresh water deeper than 1 m or keep it submerged for more than 30 minutes. If you plunge the device in any liquid other than fresh water, such as salt water, ionized water, or alcoholic beverage, liquid will enter the device faster.

- Avoid exposing the device to **water moving with force**.

- If the device is exposed to fresh water, dry it carefully with a clean, soft cloth. If the device is exposed to other liquids, such as salt water, swimming pool water, soapy water, oil, perfume, sunscreen, hand cleaner, or chemical products such as cosmetics, rinse it with fresh water and dry it painstakingly with a clean, soft cloth. Failure to follow these instructions may affect the device's performance and appearance.

- **If the device has been submerged in water or the microphone or speaker is wet,** you may have problems hearing sound clearly during a call. After wiping the device with a dry cloth, dry it painstakingly before using it.

- The device's touchscreen plus other features may malfunction **if the device is used in water.**

- **A severe fall of a hard impact on the device** may damage the water- and dust-resistant features of the device.

- Your smartphone has been duly tested in a controlled environment and under specific conditions, and consequently certified to be water- and dust-resistant. (It has satisfied the requirements of classification IP67 as defined by the international standard IEC 60529-Degrees of Protection provided by Enclosures [IP Code]; test conditions: 15-35 °C, 86-106 kPa, fresh water, 1 meter, 30 minutes). Notwithstanding this classification, there is yet the possible for your device to be damaged in certain conditions.

Instructional icons

Warning: circumstances that could cause injury to yourself or others

Caution: circumstances that could cause damage to your device or other equipment

Note: notes, usage tips, or additional information

Device overheating situations and solutions

When the device overheats during the process of charging the battery

In the process of charging, the device and its charger may become hot. It may even feel hotter to the touch during wireless charging or fast charging. This is normal and does not affect the device's lifespan or performance. If the battery becomes excessively hot, the charging speed may decrease or the charger may stop charging.

Do the following when the device heats up:

- Remove the device from the charger and close any running apps. Wait for the device to cool down and then resume charging the device again.

- If the lower part of the device overheats, it may be that the USB cable connected is damaged. Simply replace the damaged USB cable with a new Samsung-approved one.

- If you use a wireless charger for your device, never place foreign objects, such as metallic objects, magnets, and magnetic stripe cards, amid the device and the wireless charger.

NOTE: The wireless charging or fast charging feature is limited to only supported models.

When the device heats up during use

When using features or apps that utilize more power or use them for extended periods, your device may temporarily heat up because of increased battery consumption. Close any running apps and allow the device to cool down for a while.

The following are examples of circumstances in which the device may overheat. Since your device's functions and apps may vary, the examples below may not apply to your model.

- During the initial setup after purchase or when restoring data • When downloading large files

- When using apps that require more power or using apps for prolonged periods:

  − When playing high-quality games for prolonged periods

- When recording videos for prolonged periods
- When streaming videos with the device set to the maximum brightness setting
- When connecting to a TV

- When the device is doing multiple tasks concurrently (or, when running many apps in the background):
  - When using Multi window.
  - When you're updating or installing apps and recording videos at the same time.
  - When you're downloading large files while making a video call
  - When recording videos and at the same time, using a navigation app

- When you're making use of large amount of data for syncing your accounts with, for instance, the cloud or email.
- When using a navigation app in a car and you place the device in direct sunlight
- When the device's mobile hotspot and tethering feature is in use
- When the device being used in areas where there is weak signals or poor reception.
- When the device's battery is being charged with a damaged USB cable

- When the smartphone's multipurpose jack is damaged or unprotected against foreign materials, such as liquid, dust, metal powder, and pencil lead
- When you're roaming

Do the following when the device heats up:

- Always keep the device updated with the latest software.
- If there's conflicts between running apps, it may cause the device to heat up. Restart the device.
- Deactivate the Wi-Fi, GPS, and Bluetooth features when they are not in use.
- Close apps that increase battery consumption or that run in the background whenever they're not in use.
- Delete unnecessary files or unused apps.
- Decrease the brightness of the screen.
- If the device overheats or feels hot for an extended period, do not use it for a while. If the overheating persists, contact a Samsung Service Centre.

Precautions for device overheating

If you begin to feel uncomfortable as a result of the device overheating, stop using the device.

When the device heats up, limited features and performance may ensue or the device may turn off to cool down. The feature is only available on supported models.

- If the device overheats and reaches a certain temperature, you'll receive a warning message to prevent device failure, skin irritations and damages, and battery leakage. To bring down the temperature of the device, the screen brightness will be reduced, the performance speed will be limited and battery charging will stop. Also, any running apps will be closed and all calling and other features will be limited, except for emergency calls, till when the device cools down.

- If you receive the second message due to a further increase of the device's temperature, the device will turn off automatically. Allow the device's temperature to cool down below the specified level before using the device. If you receive the second warning message during an emergency call, the call will not be disconnected by a forced shut down.

Precautions for operating environment

Your device may heat up as a result of extreme weather conditions in the surrounding environment. Beware of the following conditions and take care to avoid shortening the battery's lifespan, damaging the device, or causing a fire:

- Do not keep your device in very cold or very hot temperatures.

- Do not expose your device to direct sunlight for prolonged periods.

- Do not use or keep your device for prolonged periods in very hot areas, such as inside a car during the summertime.

- Avoid placing the device in any areas that may overheat, such as on an electric heating mat.

- Never keep your device near or in heaters, microwaves, hot cooking equipment, or high-pressure containers.

- Do not use a naked or damaged cable, and do not use any charger or battery that is either damaged or malfunctioning.

CHAPTER 14
TROUBLESHOOTING TIPS

Before you eventually contact a Samsung Service Centre, please try the following solutions, although some conditions may not apply to your device.

You may also find Samsung Members handy to solve any problems you might experience while using your device.

When your device prompts you to enter one of the following codes while using it or when you turn on the device:

- Password: If you have enabled the device lock feature, you must enter the password you set for the device.

- PIN: When you want to use your smartphone for the first time or when you enable the PIN requirement, you must enter the PIN supplied with the SIM or USIM card. However, you can disable the feature by simply using the Lock SIM card menu.

- PUK: This means your SIM or USIM card has been blocked, usually because you have entered your PIN incorrectly several times. You must enter the PUK supplied with SIM or USIM card by your service provider.

- PIN2: When you access a menu that needs the PIN2, you must enter the PIN2 supplied with the SIM or USIM card. For more information about this issue, contact your service provider.

If your device is showing network or service error messages

- This usually happens as a result of weak signals or poor reception, making your device to lose reception. Try move away from your current area to another area. While moving, error messages may show again severally.
- You need a subscription to access some options in your device or its apps. For further information, contact your service provider.

Your device refuses to turn on

When the battery is utterly discharged, your device will not turn on. Charge the battery fully before turning on the device.

The touchscreen does not respond properly or is responding slowly.

- This may be as a result of a screen protector or other optional accessories attached to the touchscreen.
- If you're putting on hand gloves, if your hands are not clean while touching the touchscreen, or if you're tapping the screen with your fingertips or with sharp objects, the touchscreen may not function properly.
- The touchscreen may not function well in humid conditions or when it is exposed to water. So ensure the touchscreen is clean and dry.
- Restart your device to be sure it's cleared of any temporary software bugs.
- Confirm that your device software is updated to the latest version.

- If you have your device's touchscreen scratched or damaged, visit a Samsung Service Centre.

Your device freezes or experiences a fatal error

Experiment the following solutions. If the problem persists, contact a Samsung Service Centre.

Restarting the device

If your device is freezing or hanging intermittently, you may need to close all open apps or turn off the device and turn it on again.

Forcing restart

If your device is frozen and unresponsive, press and hold the Side key and the Volume Down key together at the same time for more than 7 seconds to restart it.

Resetting the device

If the methods above do not solve your problem, do a factory data reset.

Start the **Settings** app and click **General management** → **Reset** → **Factory data reset** → **Reset** → **Delete all**. Before performing the factory data reset, make sure you have a backup copy of important data stored in your device.

Calls are not connected

- Confirm that you have accessed the right cellular network.

- Check if you have set call barring for the phone number you are dialing. If you have done so, your call will not connect.

- Confirm that you have not set call barring for the incoming phone number.

Others cannot hear you when making a call

- Make sure that you do not cover the built-in microphone by any means.
- Make sure that you place the microphone close to your mouth.
- If you're using an earphone, make sure that it is properly connected.

You hear sound echoes during a call

Regulate the volume by pressing the Volume key or move to another area.

A cellular network or the Internet is frequently disconnected or poor audio quality

- Make sure that you're not blocking the device's internal antenna.
- When you are in areas where there are weak signals or poor reception, you may lose reception. Problems of connectivity may be associated with the service provider's base station. Change your location and try again.
- When you are using the device while moving, wireless network services may be disabled as a result of problems with the service provider's network.

The battery doesn't charge well (For Samsung-approved chargers)

- Make sure the charger is connected properly.

- Visit a Samsung Service Centre for a replacement of the battery.

The battery depletes faster than when you first purchased it

- Exposure of the device or the battery to very cold or very hot temperatures, may reduce the useful charge.
- Consider the apps and other features you use. Battery consumption increases with certain features or apps, such as GPS, games, or the Internet.
- The battery is expendable and the useful charge reduces over time. Consider replacing your expended battery.

Error messages pop up when launching the camera

You must have enough available memory and battery power to operate the camera app. If you get error messages when starting the camera, try the following:

- Charge the battery.
- Free up some space in your memory by transferring files to a computer or deleting files from your device.
- Restart the device. If the problem still persists with the camera app after trying these tips, contact a Samsung Service Centre.

Picture quality is poorer than the preview

- The quality of your pictures depends on the surroundings and the photography techniques you apply.
- Taking pictures in dark areas, at night, or indoors may cause image noise or make images to be captured out of focus.

Error messages pop up when opening multimedia files

If you receive error messages or you're unable to play multimedia files on your device, try the following:

- Free up some space in your device memory by transferring files to a computer or deleting files from your device.
- Check if the music file is Digital Rights Management (DRM)-protected. If it is, you must provide the appropriate license or key to play the file.
- Make sure that the file formats are supported by your device. If the file format is not supported, such as DivX or AC3, install the relevant app that supports it. To check the file formats that your device supports, visit the Samsung website.
- Your device supports pictures and videos that are captured with it. Pictures and videos captured by other devices may not be supported.
- Your device supports multimedia files that are authenticated by your network service provider or providers of additional services. You may have problems working with some content from the Internet, such as ringtones, videos, or wallpapers.

Bluetooth is not working well

Another Bluetooth device may be located or there may be connection problems or performance malfunctions. Otherwise, try the following:

- Make sure the device you want to connect with is ready to be scanned or connected to.

- Make sure that your device and the other Bluetooth device are within the maximum Bluetooth range which is 10m.
- On your device, start the **Settings** app, click **Connections**, and then click the **Bluetooth** switch to activate again.
- On your device, start the **Settings** app, click **General management** → **Reset** → **Reset network settings** → **Reset settings** → **Reset** to reset network settings. Your registered information may be lost when performing the reset.

If the above tips do not resolve the problem, contact a Samsung Service Centre.

The screen brightness adjustment bar does not show on the notification panel

Open the notification panel by pulling the status bar downwards, and then pull the notification panel downwards. Click ⋮ → **Quick panel layout** and click the **Show brightness control above notifications** switch to activate it.

Unable to established a connection when you connect the device to a computer

- Make sure you are using a compatible USB cable with your device.
- Make sure you have the proper driver installed on your computer and that it's up-to-date.

Your device cannot find your current location

GPS signals may be obstructed by buildings or other conditions in some locations. In such circumstances, set the device to use Wi-Fi or a mobile network to find your current location.

Data stored in the device has been lost

Always have a backup copy of every important data stored in the device. Otherwise, you cannot bring back your data if it is corrupted or lost. Samsung will not be held accountable for the loss of data stored in the device.

A small gap shows around the outside of the device case

- This gap is an essential manufacturing feature and some slight rocking or vibration of parts may take place.
- With the lapse of time, friction between parts may lead to slight expansion of this gap.

There is insufficient space in the device's storage

Delete any redundant data, such as cache, by making use of the device care feature or you can manually delete fallow apps or files to free up storage space.

The Home button does not appear

The navigation bar which contains the Home button may disappear when using some apps or features. To view the navigation bar, pull upwards from the bottom of the screen.

Removing the battery

- If you want to remove the battery for any reason, contact an authorized service center. To get instructions on how to remove battery, please visit **www.samsung.com/global/ecodesign energy**.

- For your safety, you **must not try to remove** the battery by yourself. If the battery is not properly removed, it may result in damage to the battery and/or device, cause personal injury, and/or result in the device being unsafe to use.

- Samsung does not accept any legal responsibility for any damage or loss (whether in contract or tort, including negligence) which may ensue from failure to exactly follow these warnings and instructions, save for death or personal injury caused by Samsung's negligence.

INDEX

About phone, **202**
Accessibility, **201**
Add contacts, **75**
Albums, **115**
App permission, **52**
Apps screen, **55**
AR Doodle, **123**
AR Emoji Stickers, **122**
AR Emoji Studio, **118**
AR Zone, **117**
Back up, **28**
Backup, **187**
backup data, **28**
Battery, **195**, **196**, **222**
Block numbers, **73**
Bluetooth, **141**
Calendar, **129**
Camera, **83**
Care, **195**
Connecting to a computer, **159**
Copy, **69**
Copying and pasting, **69**

Create folders, **59**
Data saver, **146**
Delete contacts, **77**
Delete folder, **60**
Deleting images, **117**
Digital Wellbeing, **194**
Display, **162**, **165**, **169**
Dual rec mode, **94**
Dust resistance, **207**
Edge panel, **61**
Emergency call, **22**
Emergency mode, **22**
Emoji, **118**
eSIM, **11**, **14**
Face recognition, **30**
Files, **132**
Fingerprint, **33**
Fingerprint recognition, **33**
Food mode, **100**
Forcing restart, **21**, **217**
Fun mode, **96**

224

Galaxy, **128**
Galaxy Store, **50**
Galaxy Wearable, **128**
Gallery, **111**
Game, **134**
Google apps, **136**
Grouping, **112**
Home screen, **55**, **167**
Hotspot, **148**
Hyperlapse, **103**
ID, **24**
Indicator icons, **62**
Intelligent features, **104**
Internet, **80**
Keyboard, **67**
Keyboard functions, **69**
Link to Windows, **158**
Lock screen, **61**, **167**
Macro mode, **101**
Making calls, **71**
Media playback, **66**
Memory, **197**
Messages, **78**
Messenger, **193**
Mobile Hotspot, **148**

Modes, **181**
Motions and gestures, **191**
Music Share, **154**
Nano-SIM card, **11**
Navigation bar. *See* Soft buttons
NFC, **144**
Night mode, **100**
Notifications, **161**
Overheating, **209**
Panorama mode, **100**
Parental control, **128**
Parental controls, **194**
Paste, **69**
Photo mode, **90**
Play Store, **51**
Portrait mode, **95**
Precautions, **204**, **212**, **213**
Printing, **149**
Pro mode, **97**
Quick setting, **65**
Quick Share, **151**
Receiving calls, **73**
Recorder, **131**

Remastering images, **113**
Reminder, **130**
Restart, **21**
Restarting, **217**
Samsung account, **23**, **24**, **48**, **161**
Samsung Cloud, **188**
Samsung Health, **125**
Samsung Kids, **127**
Samsung Notes, **126**
Samsung Pass, **47**, **172**
Samsung Pay, **38**, **39**
Screen record, **110**
Screenshot, **108**
SD card, **15**
Secure Folder, **173**, **177**
Secure Wi-Fi, **178**
Selfies, **92**, **105**
Setup, **23**
Share, **151**, **154**
Sharing contacts, **77**
SIM card, **14**
Slow motion, **102**

Smart Lock, **168**
Smart Switch, **25**
SmartThings, **157**
Soft buttons, **54**
Soundechoes, **218**
Sounds and vibration, **183**
Storage, **197**
Submerged, **208**
Super Slow-mo mode, **101**
Syncing, **116**
Transferring data. *See* Smart switch
Troubleshooting, **215**
Uninstall, **51**
Update, **202**
USIM card. *See* Nano-SIM card
Video call effects, **192**
Water resistance, **207**
Wearable, **128**
Wi-Fi, **139**
Wi-Fi Direct, **141**